Lovebirds

Their Care and Breeding

David Alderton, BA

Series Editor
Dennis Kelsey-Wood

 Books Ltd, Edlington,
Horncastle, Lincs, England

First Published 1979
by K & R Books Ltd,
Edlington, Lincolnshire

ISBN 0 903264 39 0
Cover Photograph: Fischer's Lovebird (*Agapornis fischeri*).

Typeset by Woolaston Parker Ltd, and printed by Litho Letterpress Service, both of Leicester, England, and bound in Great Britain by Hunter & Foulis Ltd, of Edinburgh

Contents

Dedication

To Joan and Eric, Michael, Martha and my other Cambridge colleagues.

Particular thanks to Michael for the line illustrations, also to Tom, Rita, Graham and Lola.

List of Illustrations

Colour

Line illustrations

Black and White

Chapter 1

Introduction

Lovebirds are an attractive group of birds belonging to the Parrot family. Although budgerigars are sometimes referred to incorrectly as lovebirds, there is no connection between the budgerigar which is a parrakeet, and the lovebird which is a true parrot. There are nine species in their genus *Agapornis*, and in total fifteen forms have been identified. Lovebirds are found exclusively in Africa and on a few of the surrounding islands, where they wander in search of the seeds and fruit which form the basis of their diet. These birds are rarely found far from water, and often travel in small groups. All lovebirds have a variable amount of green plumage which is augmented with a possible combination of red, black, yellow, orange or blue feathering, often on their heads and short tails.

The name 'lovebird' was given to these birds because of their habit of sitting close together at every opportunity, while the French and Germans refer to them as 'inseparables'. There is however no truth in the story that if one member of a pair dies, the other will follow with a broken heart. Under such circumstances, an infection of some kind should be suspected as being the underlying cause of death. Although it is certainly preferable to house these birds in pairs, one lovebird can if necessary live quite happily on its own.

Lovebirds as Pets
Lovebirds do not make such good pets as do other members of the parrot family, unless they are obtained at a very early age. It may then be possible with patience to encourage a baby lovebird to become finger-tame and talk, but it would need to be kept away from other lovebirds. There are records of a few lovebirds which have been taught to say several words by their owners. A pair of

lovebirds are not expensive to keep, and they may breed if they are housed in a suitable cage. A mixture of seeds and water, plus some fruit and green stuff given daily will satisfy their requirements, along with a regular supply of grit and cuttlefish bone which can be purchased from the shop where the seed is obtained. The call of a pair of lovebirds is generally inoffensive, unlike those of many larger parrots. Most people will not find it disturbing in the confined surroundings of a room, and furthermore lovebirds are not particularly messy in the home.

It should be safe to allow the lovebirds out of their cage providing all windows in the room are closed and covered with a net curtain, because otherwise the birds may not see the glass and attempt to fly straight through it. Other possible hazards, such as fish tanks or chimneys must also be closed off before the birds are released from their cage. The exercise will help to keep the lovebirds fit, but they should not be left alone when they are flying about the room because of the risk of injury. If they get entangled in material for example, a leg could easily be damaged. The lovebirds may well need to be caught and returned to their cage on the first few occasions that they are loose in the room. After this they will probably return to the cage of their own accord.

Lovebirds as Aviary Occupants

These birds show to best advantage in an outside aviary, and here they score over most of their relations in the parrot family. Lovebirds do not require elaborate accommodation, being quite content to live and breed in an aviary of modest dimensions. They are therefore ideal occupants for an aviary in a small back garden, and will not make much more noise than a pair of budgerigars. The lovebirds will obviously be more active in such larger quarters rather than a cage, and breeding is more likely to be successful out of doors.

A well-planned aviary can be an attractive addition to any garden, and provides considerable scope for the imaginative gardener. Many plants are suitable for growing around the aviary, out of reach of the birds, but sadly any within the enclosure will be destroyed by the lovebirds. Quick-growing annuals, such as nasturtiums or convolvulus sown as seed may be trained up the shelter sides which are visible from the house, and their flowers

9

each-faced Lovebird (Agapornis roseicollis).

provide a mass of colour during the summer. An aviary which is well maintained should last for years, and yet providing it is built in sections bolted together, moving the structure and re-erecting it will not present too many problems.

Rather like the dove which is incorrectly but universally accepted as a bird of peace, lovebirds will usually fight if they are housed together in a group. Fighting is particularly likely when the birds are in breeding condition, and it is much safer to house individual pairs in separate aviaries. Lovebirds are also not suitable for mixing with other birds, unless the aviary is exceptionally large, and even then fights may still develop on occasions. They are quite capable of breaking the legs of small seed eaters, in addition to mutilating larger birds like budgerigars.

When the lovebirds are breeding, their antics are especially interesting to watch. Unlike the vast majority of the parrot tribe, lovebirds not only use nesting material to construct a nest, but some species such as the Peach-faced have a fascinating way of tucking suitable pieces of bark and other material in amongst their body feathers. In the Peach-faced, the feathers of the back and rump are specialised for this purpose, and only in the Hanging Parrots (*Loriculus*) has a similar adaptation been noted.

The first sight of the young lovebirds when they leave the nestbox never fails to delight even the most experienced aviculturist. The satisfaction obtained by breeding from these chicks is even greater, and in this way a strain of aviary-bred birds can be established. Breeding of stock is necessary to ensure the continued existence of today's species in captivity, because already some, such as the Red-faced and Madagascar which were formerly common, have virtually disappeared from collections.

None of the lovebirds at present, with the possible exception of the Black-collared Lovebird, about which little is known, can be described as rare in the wild, and in some areas they are regarded as pest species. A few years ago for example, Tanzania was suffering from a plague of lovebirds, and rather than having to continue outlaying large sums of money on destroying thirty thousand birds annually, the government preferred to send them to aviculturists abroad. They realised however that for the scheme to be successful, the lovebirds would have to arrive at their destinations in good condition, and so their export was controlled by the Government Veterinary Service. Such numbers of birds are unlikely to be available to breeders again, and with increasing pressure on wildlife throughout Africa, further restrictions on the trade in lovebirds can be envisaged.

Mutations
As lovebirds are more often bred in captivity these days, it is not surprising that a range of mutations or 'sports' have also appeared. Strains of these birds have been carefully developed, and the result is an even greater interest in lovebirds over the past few years, reminiscent of the enthusiasm which greeted the early budgerigar mutations. Healthy mutation lovebirds do not pose any additional problems with regard to care, but they are more expensive than normals, and perhaps the beginner is wiser to gain some experience in breeding normal lovebirds before keeping the mutations. The mutations should become available in ever increasing numbers in the future, as more will be bred each year.

Imported and Home Bred Stock
As already suggested, the number of imported lovebirds available has fallen dramatically over several years, following the introduction of both export and import restrictions. This in turn has led to an increase in their price, and a shift in emphasis towards the development of captive-bred strains. Some lovebirds such as the Masked have bred quite freely in captivity, and so surplus birds are often available especially in the autumn after the breeding season. Any of the White eye-ringed type or the Peach-faced Lovebird are suitable for the beginner who hopes to breed from his birds, since this group are usually quite keen to produce a family. However other lovebirds, particularly the Red-faced and Madagascar, have proved difficult to breed and so it may be necessary to purchase imported stock of these species.

Imported birds should be avoided if possible because they are unlikely to be fully acclimatised, and their age will be completely unknown unless they are in immature plumage. Problems associated with changing their diet may also arise, and although lovebirds imported into Britain will have been quarantined for at least thirty-five days, there is still an increased risk of introducing parasites and disease from these birds to established stock.

How to Purchase Lovebirds

Lovebirds can be obtained from breeders and dealers who advertise in the columns of the weekly magazine *Cage and Aviary Birds*. Another possibility is to contact a local bird club, because this will invariably yield the address of someone who breeds lovebirds in the area. Indeed, membership of a club provides a useful opportunity to discuss successes and problems with other breeders in friendly surroundings.

It is always advisable to arrange a convenient time to call on the vendor, rather than purchasing birds by letter or a telephone call. Apart from seeing the surroundings of the lovebirds, a visit enables one to choose the birds personally, possibly guided by the advice of an experienced fancier, and this can be especially valuable when there are a number for sale. It is worth asking if the lovebirds have been kept outside, and whether or not they have bred, as well as enquiring about their age and diet. In some cases, it will be necessary to rely on the vendor's honesty, and then the birds will have to be purchased without being seen beforehand. Under these circumstances, a dealer will dispatch the lovebirds by train, on receipt of payment and the rail fee. The birds are then collected from a local station, but it is advisable to check in advance that the particular station handles livestock. They will probably telephone as soon as the birds arrive, so a telephone number should be included if possible with the address when the lovebirds are ordered. Most firms guarantee live delivery, and a few are sufficiently confident in their stock to operate an approval system whereby the birds can be returned by the customer, whose money is refunded if they are not satisfied with them on arrival.

General Points about Choosing Good Stock

Healthy lovebirds ought to be both tight feathered and alert, and those which do not move from their perch when the cage is approached are rarely fit. In addition, there should be no staining around the vent, and the eyes and nostrils of the bird must be free from discharge. Examination of the feet will reveal if any claws are missing. Although the absence of claws will not affect the breeding potential of the lovebird, it will make the bird unsuitable for showing at a later date. Unfortunate specimens with more severe handicaps, such as droopy wings or defective beaks

*Yellow and Green Pied Peach-faced Lovebird (*Agapornis roseicollis*).
A predominantly yellow example, but darker in colour than a normal
yellow. Crossings with the Golden Cherry variety have yielded Double
Yellows which show both shades of yellow on the same bird.*

should not be acquired as these faults may prevent breeding from being successful.

The condition of the lovebird's feathers is especially important, because plucking is a particular vice of these birds. Observations suggest that this complaint may be inherited in some cases, and so any birds with areas of down feathers, or even worse, those with bare skin visible ought to be avoided. A further consideration is that lovebirds which are plucked in the nest generally prove wilder than usual when adult. Even when fully feathered it is therefore unlikely that they will make good show specimens. The position is however complicated in the case of the Abyssinian Lovebird, since the hen plucks some of her feathers which are then used as nesting material, and so when in breeding condition, she may appear remarkably bald.

Young healthy stock must therefore be acquired to ensure a good start in the hobby. Poor aged specimens will turn out to be a liability even if they are housed and fed correctly. Many breeders will sell some progeny from their most reliable pairs, but they will not often part with breeding stock. Buying young lovebirds should provide the best chance of success in the following year, because they are given time to settle in their new quarters before being expected to breed. A major disadvantage however is that most immature lovebirds are even harder to sex than adults, and the best course is to buy several if possible, allowing them to pair off themselves. Surplus birds can then be sold readily just before the next breeding season. There is a great temptation to purchase the first pair of lovebirds which are seen, but they should only be bought if they satisfy the criteria discussed above, because otherwise disappointment may well ensue.

Chapter 2

History

The Red-faced Lovebird was probably the first species brought to Europe by Portuguese travellers back in the sixteenth century. Large numbers of these lovebirds followed at intervals right up until the 1960's. In spite of this the species is very rarely offered for sale in Britain today, although examples are still imported into Portugal and Spain.

Lovebirds became more regularly available during the late nineteenth century. A large number of Madagascar Lovebirds were imported at this time, and a pair first bred for certain in England in 1882, but there is a record of these birds being bred ten years earlier in Germany. Later in 1890, the magazine *Die Gefiederte Welt* reported that a Madagascar Lovebird had bred successfully with a budgerigar producing hybrid offspring, but this would be a most exceptional result. The Peach-faced Lovebird was bred earlier in 1869 by Dr. Brehm in Germany, and as soon as it became known in Europe, a ready demand sprang up for this attractive species.

Abyssinian Lovebirds were irregularly available in the later years of the last century. They were bred for the first time in 1911 by an aviculturist from Vienna, and an account again appeared in *Die Gefiederte Welt*. These species had been joined by imports of the Black-cheeked Lovebird just before the First World War in 1908. It did not prove a very popular species, and faded from the avicultural scene until 1926 when the Nyasa Lovebird also became available for the first time. The Masked Lovebird, discovered in 1877, had reached Europe in the previous year, and Fischer's Lovebirds were first seen in Britain during the mid-twenties.

Budgerigar mutations were becoming freely available at this time, and there was a great upsurge of interest in breeding birds.

Some species of lovebird proved quite keen to breed, and their popularity rose with that of the budgerigar so large numbers were brought into the country. However, this initial interest was not sustained, and by the time a ban was imposed on the import of parrotlike birds in 1930, lovebird prices had plummeted to a low level. During these early years, the requirements of lovebirds were not fully understood and they were kept in unsuitable conditions. It is little wonder that lovebirds were condemned as aggressive troublemakers when they were kept in aviaries with budgerigars. The problems of sexing encountered with some species led to disappointing breeding results, while the sexually dimorphic species proved difficult, if not impossible to breed in captivity as in the case of the Red-faced Lovebird.

Some aviculturists still remained loyal to the genus, and as these breeders observed their birds, they were able to gain a clearer idea of their needs. Breeding results began to improve and interest in the group was rekindled during the late 1930's.

However Europe was again divided by war in 1939 and hardly surprisingly, people's attention once more turned away from lovebirds to more pressing matters. The dwindling stocks of seed had to be eked out with other, often poorer foodstuffs. Some species proved more adaptable than others. Nyasa and Black-cheeked Lovebirds had almost vanished completely by the end of the war. Yet the Peach-faced and Masked species stood their ground, and the Fischer's Lovebirds proved very adaptable to the harsher conditions. Much of the stock which survived the war had been hybridised, to such an extent that it is doubtful if many pure Black Masked Lovebirds remained in the country, following crossings with the Black-cheeked Lovebird.

The parrot ban was lifted in 1952, and new stock again became available. Attention was to be focused on establishing pure strains, and some breeders specialised in breeding the colour mutations. The latest restrictions affecting the importation of birds came into force in March 1976, and while there is not a complete ban on imports, rigorous quarantine regulations have increased the prices of all birds. This however has had a beneficial effect by stimulating an increased interest in the breeding of lovebirds, although some species have disappeared from the advertisement columns of the avicultural magazines. It is highly unlikely that lovebirds such as the Madagascar will be

16

available to aviculturists again in the foreseeable future, and further restrictions can be anticipated.

While budgerigars are now available in a wide range of colours mutations have also been developed in the more free breeding species of lovebirds. They first appeared when a wild Blue Masked Lovebird was sent to England in 1927, and this saw the beginnings of attempts to build up a blue strain. A pair of these birds was first shown by Miss de Pledge at Crystal Palace in 1934. Blue Masked Lovebirds were bred in California around 1932, from imported stock which presumably must have been split for blue. The existing European strain of blues subsequently benefited from the introduction of this American blood.

Once the Yellow Masked Lovebird had been bred in America, about 1935, it was then possible using this mutation in conjunction with Blue Masked birds to breed whites. This latter colour appeared initially in Japan at the time of the Second World War. White Masked Lovebirds still have a blue tinge to their body plumage, and a faint mask. Albinos will only be bred when a Lutino Masked Lovebird is established. Crossing a Blue Masked cock with a Lutino hen, and then pairing the resulting normal cocks, which will carry both lutino and blue factors, to Blue hens should result in albinos making their appearance for the first time. If these colours prove to be sex-linked (as explained later), then hens cannot be split for either lutino or albino.

In the case of the Peach-faced Lovebird, a true albino will probably be bred in the very near future. Pastel Blue Peach-faced Lovebirds, which are now quite common, are not in fact pure blues because they retain some pink coloration on the head and throat. These birds, when used like the Blue Masked, produce attractive yellowy-cream offspring, also with pink facial markings which are sometimes referred to as Cream-albinos.

Cream Peach-faced Lovebirds are not strictly albinos, because some colour pigment is retained, but now with the very recent breeding in Europe of genuine Blue Peach-faced Lovebirds with white faces, it should be possible to breed albinos. In addition, it has been reported from Switzerland that Pastel Cobalt and Mauve Peach-faced Lovebirds have been bred, by introducing the dark factor from Jade and Olive birds, and they were named by the colour of their rumps. The Olive variety first appeared in Australia about 1968, where Alan Hollingsworth of Victoria was one of the

first breeders. Pastel Blues have also been used to produce the Silver Cherry (White) variety, when paired with the Golden Cherry (Yellow) Peach-faced which originated in Japan in 1954. The young from this pairing when mated back to Pastel Blues produce Whites.

The original Pied Peach-faced Lovebirds had variable areas of bright yellow plumage set against green, and this has proved to be a dominant mutation. The pied factor has subsequently been introduced into Pastel Blues, yielding less-colourful pieds which retain areas of a slight yellow appearance rather than white, because the Pastel Blue, as mentioned earlier is not a pure blue. Pied Pastel Cobalts and Mauves will doubtless emerge shortly, but only when the Blue Peach-faced is established will Blue and White Pied Peach-faced Lovebirds be bred. Yellow pieds have occasionally been reported in other species, but probably result from nutritional and metabolic errors. In the case of the Masked Lovebird, however, Vane describes specimens of the Yellow Masked variety as being yellow and green pieds, rather than yellows, and these birds are proven recessives.

Mutations are not yet as common in other species of *Agapornis*, although Blue and Yellow Fischer's for example have been bred. Ronald Horsham of Cape Town, South Africa, noticed that some Fischers, in his possession in 1957, descended from pure wild-caught stock, had more orange on their breasts than normal and so he set out to breed either orange or red specimens. No red chicks were forthcoming, but he was surprised to find in a nest of four that there were three blue chicks. These Blues, with their grey heads, differed significantly from the Blue Masked mutation. He kept his birds on a colony system, and found that when the Blues paired together, a high proportion of the eggs were infertile, probably because his stock was too closely related.

The Lutino Nyasa Lovebird, another member of the White eye-ringed group was first bred by Mr. Prendergast of Adelaide, Australia, in 1933. It has proved to be an autosomal recessive mutation, and not a sex-linked recessive as is more usual with lutino mutations. Very few Lutino Nyasa Lovebirds are now seen in Europe as their numbers have fallen quite dramatically, yet breeders such as Vane were successful with this mutation after the war.

Colour variations have also been observed in the sexually dimorphic group of lovebirds, but are less likely to occur because

Albino Peach-faced Lovebird. The most recent form bred from blue ancestry.

significantly fewer birds of these species are bred in captivity. A wild-caught Abyssinian Lovebird with some brown flight feathers was kept by George Smith, while Lutino Red-faced Lovebirds will remain probably the rarest of all *Agapornis* mutations. There is sadly little prospect of the latter type ever becoming widely available because of the problems inherent in breeding this species. Overall, however, the exciting development of lovebird mutations is bound to continue over the next few years, hopefully without the use of hybrids.

Chapter 3

Accommodation

The type of accommodation provided for lovebirds varies greatly from owner to owner. Lovebirds kept as pets are often housed in cages although some people prefer to wire off an area of a room, and so form an indoor flight for their birds. The serious breeder however will endeavour to house his stock in outside aviaries which are designed with the needs of the birds uppermost in his mind. Such breeders will also require cages at times and since most people begin by keeping a bird in a cage, it seems appropriate to begin this chapter with a consideration of cages suitable for lovebirds.

Cages
Lovebirds are housed in cages either of an all-wire design or a box-type construction. All-wire cages provide perhaps the most decorative means of displaying lovebirds in the home, but from the bird's viewpoint, such cages can leave much to be desired. By their very nature, they provide no cover or seclusion for the bird. In the wild, most lovebirds when not feeding or on the wing seek some sort of protection. It is not surprising therefore that a bird will fly madly around an all-wire cage when approached, especially if the surroundings are unfamiliar. The siting of this type of cage is important, not only to give the lovebird a sense of security, but also because it is easily exposed to draughts which may result in chills. Such a cage should ideally be located in a well-lit corner of the room, out of direct sunlight and draughts.

The lovebirds can be viewed best if the cage is positioned at eye-level, and a further advantage is that at this height, mischievous young hands should not be able to pull the cage over or open the door. The bars of parrot cages are too widely spaced to house a lovebird safely. The bird will struggle to get its head between the bars, particularly when frightened, and may get stuck or even kill itself. A larger than average budgerigar cage, with a length of at least 2 feet (61 cm.) is satisfactory for lovebirds. If a stand is necessary, it is advisable to choose the heaviest model available.

Cage breeding is much more likely to be successful if the lovebirds are housed in a box-type cage, because this gives them greater seclusion. A budgerigar breeding cage, again at least 2 feet (61 cm) in length, 18 inches (46 cm) wide and 18 inches (46 cm) high is ideal, and these cages often have nestboxes attached. These nestboxes are quite suitable for lovebirds, although the entrance hole may be on the small side for some species, and if so it will need to be enlarged.

The interior of such a cage is often very dark, but this can be overcome by painting the inside with a light emulsion paint. White is perhaps the most popular choice, but providing the paint

Red-faced Lovebirds (Agapornis pullaria) *will usually live together without fighting, unlike most other species.*

is non-toxic, and does not contain any lead, the actual colour is immaterial. Lovebirds have more powerful beaks than budgerigars, and they will not hesitate to whittle away any unprotected woodwork. Box cages made partially of hardboard should therefore be avoided, and all joints must be as flush as possible. Thick plywood is the most suitable material for cage construction, and since the budgerigar-type cage fronts are sold separately in a variety of sizes, it is not too difficult to make a suitable cage. The nestbox can either be made or purchased and then attached to the cage, preferably by brackets, which enable it to be removed easily.

Aviaries
Before starting to construct an aviary, it is advisable to find out if there are any planning requirements which have to be observed. Planning permission is not usually needed for an aviary, but especially if the property is rented, other restrictions may apply. Local council offices will be able to advise on the current legal position, and it is useful to take a sketch of the site when seeking advice on this matter.

Aviaries are available in many shapes and sizes, ranging from the typical rectangular design to more ornate octagonal (eight-sided) structures. The choice of aviary will depend largely as always, on the finance available. Professionally made aviaries can be purchased from many of the larger bird dealers. Although perhaps expensive, such aviaries are ideal for someone who is unable to spare the time, or lacks confidence to build their own structure. Some firms offer wired panels, doors and other components separately, and will advise on the number and type of units required to enclose a certain area. This approach allows greater flexibility, and later expansion by adding further panels is relatively easy. It is always worth planning for the future when constructing aviaries. In many cases, enthusiasm soon increases, particularly when breeding is successful, and then existing accommodation has to be enlarged.

Building one's own aviary is not a very difficult task for the handyman, providing a few basic rules are followed. It is obviously cheaper than purchasing a ready-built structure, but self-construction can have its headaches, and it will invariably take longer than intended to complete the aviary.

Above and opposite. *External views and plans of a typical aviary.*

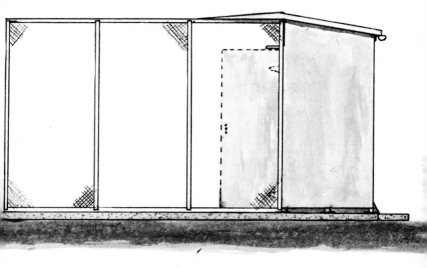

Elevation

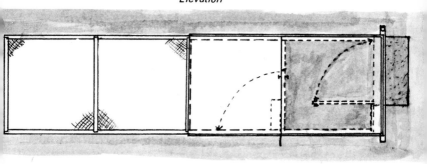

Plan

SCALE

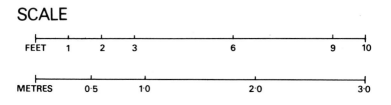

| FEET | 1 | 2 | 3 | 6 | 9 | 10 |

| METRES | 0·5 | 1·0 | 2·0 | 3·0 |

Location

The position of the aviary is an important consideration, particularly if breeding is to be successful. If it is located in an exposed position, for example, there is an increased risk of the eggs being chilled when the hen leaves the nest. The aviary should thus be sited in a relatively sheltered and quiet position, bearing in mind that much pleasure can be had from watching the lovebirds if they are visible from the house. Some shade must be provided for the birds when the sun is at its hottest, but at the same time, trees and shrubs ought not to overhang the aviary directly. Apart from reducing the light reaching the birds in winter, branches breaking off in a storm may damage the structure, and each autumn the aviary roof will be covered with leaves.

The Flight

Most aviaries are comprised of two parts, an outer flight which is largely uncovered, and an attached shelter where the lovebirds can feed and roost. Although the flight frame can be made of metal rods or pipes, it is as effective, and cheaper, to use timber 2 inches (50 mm) by 2 inches (50 mm) in width, which will form the basis of a sturdy structure. The wood certainly need not be smooth-planed and indeed when treated with preservative, rough wood gives a more pleasing rustic appearance. Second-hand wood can sometimes be purchased from demolition contractors, and reduces the cost of the aviary considerably. However, any wood used must not be warped, or infected with woodworm. Painted or varnished wood should also be avoided, in case the coating may subsequently prove harmful to the birds.

Most lovebirds need to be housed in individual pairs to prevent fighting and although a large flight is not essential, the birds are invariably fitter when more flying space is available. A suitable size for a flight is about 9 feet (2·7 metres) long, 3 feet (91 cm) wide and 6 feet (1·8 metres) high. Construction using these dimensions is easier because most aviary wire sold is 3 feet (91 cm) in width. This means that only two supporting beams, located at 3 feet (91 cm) and 6 feet (1·8 metres) along the larger sides of the rectangular frame, are required, and there will be no wastage of wire. The eventual aviary will be much more solid if the flight frames are jointed in a T-shaped manner. It is always advisable to purchase lengths of wood which are several inches longer than necessary to allow for jointing. Any excess can be cut off during construction, but it is very difficult to satisfactorily join an extra couple of inches of wood on to a length!

The wood is conveniently treated with a preservative such as creosote before being made into frames, which are more cumbersome to manage. Creosote is easily applied with a paintbrush and will not harm the birds once it has dried thoroughly. After being exposed to the air for two or three weeks, it will be quite safe. Several coats of creosote applied in succession provide the most effective treatment. When the wood is cut, then the joints and any exposed ends must also be treated.

Wire
The wire used to cover the frames should be sixteen gauge. Although thinner nineteen gauge is sometimes used for lovebirds, this is not as durable and will not be substantial enough if other species of parrots are kept later. The diameter of the wire is important if mice are to be excluded from the aviary. Mice cannot usually get through half inch by half inch (13 mm by 13 mm) wire, but this mesh is expensive. It is cheaper to purchase half inch by one inch (13 mm by 25 mm) wire which seems effective in excluding all but the smallest mice. However, any larger mesh presents no problems for these potentially harmful rodents. Substantial savings on the cost of aviary wire can be made by purchasing at the discount prices of firms which advertise in the magazine *Cage and Aviary Birds*.

The wire is simply fixed to the woodwork by means of staples available from most hardware stores. They ought to be positioned about every inch (25 mm) along the wire around the frame. The wire must be applied to the side of the frame which will form the inner face of the aviary, and should cover the wooden frame completely. This prevents the lovebirds gaining access to the woodwork which they would attack with their powerful beaks. It is useful to have some assistance when wiring the frames, because the final appearance of the aviary will be spoiled unless the wire is taut and straight on the frames. With one person nailing and the other keeping the wire taut in position, the problem should be eliminated. Some fanciers paint the aviary wire with a black emulsion paint, which helps to increase its lifespan, and makes the birds more visible. When each frame is complete, assembly is fairly straightforward especially if the relative positions of the various frames have been numbered during construction. With a separate frame for the roof, the flight will be quite sectional, and so dismantling should not be too difficult at a later date. Non-sectional aviaries are much harder to move and seldom can be re-erected with ease, which is worth remembering before purchasing a second-hand aviary.

The Shelter

It is essential for dry and draught-proof roosting quarters to be provided. Such accommodation usually takes the form of a shed-like structure attached to the flight. It can be constructed as part of the flight, and then lined with hardboard on the inside. The hardboard will not be destroyed if its edges are wired over or protected by strips of tin, and the shelter will be much lighter if the lining is painted with a white emulsion. A structure of 3 feet

A very rare cock Lutino Red-faced Lovebird (Agapornis pullaria).

28

(91 cm) long, 6 feet (1·8 metres) high and 3 feet (91 cm) wide is an ideal complement for the flight previously suggested, so that the horizontal lengths of wood must be just over 12 feet (3·6 metres) in length. In some cases, it is more convenient to make the shed unit separately, and then bolt it to the flight. On the outside, the sides and roof area should be covered preferably with tongued and grooved wood which is a most effective draught and damp excluder. The roof ought to be sloped backwards so that rain runs away from the flight. Roofing felt must be applied on top of the wood on the roof, and perhaps on the sides. A coat of tar before application of the felt helps to ensure that the structure remains waterproof, and all exposed wood is again treated with creosote.

Doors

Two doors, one entering the shelter and another leading from there into the outside flight are perhaps the most practical arrangement. The door at the back of the shelter should have a large window set in it, because the lovebirds will not enter unless the interior is well-lit. The window must be wired over because otherwise the birds may not recognise the barrier and so fly straight at the glass and injure or kill themselves. In the summer, it should be possible to open or remove this window so that there is adequate ventilation in the shelter. Any accessible woodwork must also be protected and thin one inch by half inch (25 mm by 13 mm) battening can be tacked over exposed ends of wire. It may be necessary to replace this at intervals if it is whittled away by the birds.

Some breeders like to have a door at the end of the flight opposite the shelter, often associated with a safety porch which prevents the birds escaping when the aviary is entered. If there is no attached safety porch, the door should be positioned as low as possible to reduce the risk of the lovebirds flying out of the aviary. Birds rarely fly downwards when threatened, but it can be awkward entering through a small low door especially if the weather is unpleasant! A safety porch allows the door to be positioned at a normal height, because the outer door of the wired porch is closed before the aviary is entered so that if a bird flies out, it will remain confined in the porch.

The disadvantage of a safety porch is that it requires more

space, and adds considerably to the cost of the aviary. By a relatively simple adjustment, the double doored shelter previously mentioned can be just as efficient without extra cost. A landing platform about 9 inches (22·8 cm) in width and length should be provided on the inner door as high as possible, corresponding in part to the level of the window on the outer door. The lovebirds alight on the platform, and enter through the gap. A runner extending about 1 foot (30 cm) beyond the platform, but flush with the door, is constructed. It is then possible to close the entrance hole by sliding a suitable piece of plywood along the runner into position without entering the flight. This can be achieved by attaching the plywood to a thick piece of wire running outside the flight through the aviary mesh. The birds can thus be safely confined in the outside flight, and the outer door is then opened giving access to the shelter. Once that door is closed, the inner door to the flight can be opened without fear of the birds escaping.

Site Preparation
The site will need to be marked out and levelled if necessary before work begins. The aviary will have a longer life if it is mounted on a course of bricks, and so a foundation trench about 1 foot (30 cm) deep, should be dug around its perimeter. When the trench has been filled with rubble and concrete the bricks can be laid above the level of the ground. Apart from providing support, this concrete will help to keep rodents out.

The aviary frames can then be attached to the bricks either by masonry nails, or bolts set upright in concrete between the bricks. The concrete base must be thoroughly dry before the aviary is assembled, but additional mortar can be sandwiched around the bottom of the frames in contact with the bricks during construction. The bolts around the frames should be oiled and if washers are put on before the nuts it will be much easier to dismantle the aviary later.

The Base
There are several possible coverings for the floor of an aviary. A grass floor is the most natural, but unless the aviary is very large, muddy patches will invariably develop and its appearance will be spoilt. New turves must be regarded with caution, because they

Blue Peach-faced Lovebird (Agapornis roseicollis). This, unlike the Pastel Blue, is a rare mutation at present.

may have been treated with a chemical weedkiller. Although lovebirds undoubtedly appreciate access to fresh grass, the problems associated with a grass or earth floor outweigh the advantages, especially since green food can be supplied to the birds daily.

It is very difficult to thoroughly clean the floor of a grass flight, and so the birds are more exposed to infections, especially by a variety of parasitic worms. The lovebirds may have to be washed before a show if they take to walking on a muddy floor, and this will unsettle them. Stale ground has long been associated with a decline in fertility, and a partial solution is to move the aviary to another area of grass. However, it is vital to ensure that the structure is firmly positioned in its new location so that it will not blow over in a gale.

Large gravel chips are sometimes used on the floor of outside flights, and these can be raked over, but drainage problems may occur unless the chips are several inches deep. The major concern about these two floor coverings is the ease with which rats, mice and even foxes could enter the aviary. Wire buried under the floor of the aviary will reduce this risk but it will not provide complete security.

Mice do not harm lovebirds directly, but their presence may cause night fright and then fatalities occur as the birds dash madly around the aviary. Both rats and mice present a serious disease risk, especially if they have access to the food pots. Rats and foxes may maim or kill the lovebirds and in the morning only a few feathers and a tell-tale hole in the floor will remain.

A concrete floor is perhaps the best solution, although for one reason or another it is not always practical, particularly if the aviary is only temporary. In such cases, paving slabs can be laid on the floor, and filled around with cement. About four inches (10 cm) of concrete and wire should exclude the most determined rat, and if the concrete is sloped from the sleeping quarters to the end of the flight, then drainage will be simply and effectively achieved. A concrete floor can be scraped and washed off thoroughly at intervals.

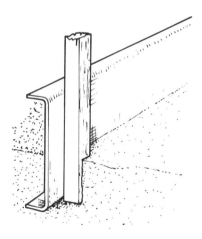

To exclude mice from an aviary, sheet metal can be nailed to the uprights and turned over above and below ground level.

The Finishing Touches

Lovebirds like to have access to the outside flight even when the weather is bad. Providing the birds are acclimatised, this is quite safe but it is advisable to provide some protection for them. Translucent plastic sheeting is often used to cover the first 3 feet (91 cm) of the flight roof, and a similar distance on the sides. However, the plastic is not very easy to cut even using a sharp hacksaw blade, and it is better to ask the store if they will cut the sheets to the required length. The sheets can be sloped on the roof so that the water runs off into the exposed part of the flight, away from the shelter. A piece of guttering fixed along the roof of the shelter helps to remove the rain falling on this area, and it can be connected to a garden water butt.

Lovebirds will destroy any greenery placed in their aviary and so it is not worth attempting to plant their flight. Perches cut from trees are however appreciated, and help to keep their beaks in trim. Stripping off the bark also occupies the birds, and natural perches in a cage may help to prevent feather plucking which can result from boredom. The perches can be cut from many trees such as apple or elderberry. However, privet, laburnum, lilac and yew must not be used because they are poisonous and for the same reason, branches ought not to be taken from any trees which have recently been sprayed with insecticides.

After being washed off, the perches are fastened in position in the aviary. Lovebirds prefer flying up and down the flight, and so perches should be arranged across it at various heights. Tree-shaped branches fixed in a large flowerpot for example on the aviary floor are always appreciated, but overhanging must be avoided if possible, because the lower perches will soon be soiled by the birds' droppings. The perches can be either bent against the aviary mesh, or better still wired on to the flight, providing no loose ends of wire protrude into the aviary. Dowelling makes suitable perches for the shelter, but it ought not to be used exclusively because its constant shape and diameter does not allow the birds to exercise their feet as they would in the wild.

Further Development

It is possible to add another unit alongside the first structure without too many problems, although it is more satisfactory to remove the established pair of lovebirds when the aviary is actually being put up. The ideal time of year for this work is therefore immediately after the breeding season, but before the weather turns cold, so that the birds can be returned to their quarters for winter. Construction is similar but now only one long flight frame will be necessary, although another layer of wire must be fixed on to the existing aviary side which is to be enclosed. Double wiring prevents lovebirds maiming each other through the mesh as they would if only a single layer of wire separated them.

If several aviaries are constructed together in this way, then it may be worth considering enclosing the area behind the shelter doors to form a corridor. This section can be used for seed storage, while shelving is useful for cages and nestboxes which are not in use. Furthermore, stock training in preparation for shows is easier, because simply walking up and down the corridor will help to steady the lovebirds, by giving them a chance to get used to people in close proximity.

Heating and lighting may also be added, although breeders' views vary on this point. Some feel that the expense is not justified, and the birds moult more often like pet budgerigars kept inside. Others point to the fact that an hour or so of additional light during the winter gives the lovebirds more opportunity to feed, and suggest that the birds reach breeding condition earlier in the following spring. Imported lovebirds usually require some heat during their first winter, but if only one pair is kept, it is easier to bring them inside rather than have the expense of arranging additional heating.

The safest method of heating a birdroom is an electrical tubular heater, similar to those used in greenhouses. With a thermostatic connection, not only is the temperature kept within a small range, but the cost is also kept to a minimum because no energy is wasted. Tubular heaters can be kept in the shelter, but they must be completely covered in a wire cage with the connecting leads inaccessible to the lovebirds. Oil or paraffin (kerosene) lamps are more dangerous, not only as a potential fire hazard, but also because of the fumes which may build up in a confined space. It is obviously not safe to have this type of heating in with the birds, and so it is not really practical for an aviary shelter.

Light bulbs and connections must also be protected from the birds in an aviary. Timing and dimming devices for lights are available so that the light level can be gradually reduced as happens in the wild. Without doubt, a low wattage bulb is useful in an aviary if the birds have to be disturbed during darkness. This may be necessary in winter, when work dictates that feeding has to be carried out either in the early morning or evening in relative darkness. The lighting timer can be set so that the aviary is lit just before feeding commences, and then the birds will not be frightened, having adjusted to the light.

Chapter 4

General Management

Lovebirds are not difficult birds to maintain, especially once they are established in their quarters. They must always have access to food and water, which is best supplied fresh each day. The water containers will need to be checked several times during the day when extremes of temperature prevail. If there is a likelihood of a severe frost, they should not be filled completely because when the water freezes, it will need space to expand or else the water container will crack and subsequently leak everywhere. During the summer, the lovebirds will drink more water, particularly when they are rearing young chicks and it may be worthwhile purchasing an additional container to ensure that they do not run short of water.

Seed for the lovebirds need not be given daily, providing there is sufficient in the food pots. Green food and soft food must be provided absolutely fresh and any which remains in the evening should be removed particularly in hot weather, because it may go sour or attract flies. All pots and water containers need to be washed regularly in mild disinfectant and then thoroughly rinsed and drained again before use.

Aviary Cleanliness
For most people, it is more convenient to clean the lovebirds and do any necessary washing at the weekends when more time is available. Good hygiene is an important part of all bird husbandry, and regular cleaning helps to prevent the spread of disease. The floor of the shelter is conveniently covered with old newspapers. Coloured sheets should be avoided because the inks used in their production may harm the lovebirds if they tear up the newspaper. Loose seed spilled on the floor is easily collected on the paper and it could be worth acquiring a winnowing machine if there is a lot

A pair of Masked Lovebirds (Agapornis personat

of wastage. This machine will separate good seed from husk so that the reclaimed seed can be supplied to the birds again. Although most winnowers on the market today are very efficient when dealing with small seeds such as canary and millet, they are not as successful when sunflower seed is included in the mixture. With one pair of lovebirds in the flight, the newspaper should be changed once or twice a week. Bird sand or peat are alternative coverings which can be used on the floor of the shelter, but they have no advantage over newspaper and increase the cost of keeping the birds. Furthermore, seed saving is not practical using these loose coverings.

The flight should also be cleaned regularly, and if the floor is concrete, it can be hosed off occasionally. Cages also will benefit from being washed at intervals and repainted as necessary. A cage may be lined with any of the coverings suggested for the floor of the shelter, but because the birds will be in closer contact with the bottom of the cage, sand is more effective under these circumstances. Regular spraying with a preparation to kill mites will reduce the risk of these parasites becoming established in the aviary.

Rats, Cats and Mice
In spite of all precautions, rodents do sometimes gain access to an aviary and then they must be eliminated without delay, partly because they breed so fast. Poison however is not safe to use within the aviary in case the lovebirds eat some of the bait. Spring traps are obviously dangerous, but as a last resort they can be placed away from the birds under a large flowerpot. The pot will also contain the vermin when there is an obvious hole in the floor through which they are entering the aviary. Some dealers stock traps which catch mice or rats alive without harming the birds in the aviary, and several rodents can be caught at one setting, which quickly reduces the population. If a hole is seen within the aviary, other holes scattered outside the aviary may be found following a careful search. Sulphur fuses can be purchased, and once lit they are placed as far as possible down the holes which are then sealed with damp cloths and a brick on top. The gas released should saturate the burrows, killing off the rodents providing there is no escape route for them.

Cats are useful when they reduce the numbers of rodents, but

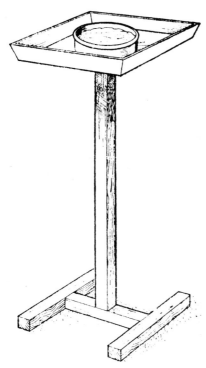

A home-made mouse-proof feeding table. Some bird keepers make this appliance with the tray inverted, but the illustrated method is preferred as it retains the seed husks and prevents spilled seed from falling to the ground and attracting mice.

they can be a problem if they climb over the aviary. Even if the cat does not injure the inmates, it may well prevent breeding from being successful, by causing hens to desert both eggs and chicks. Apart from the old solution of hurling bucketfuls of water over fleeing feline intruders, an additional layer of nineteen gauge wire, 2 inches (50 mm) by 2 inches (50 mm) fixed on to the unwired outer side of the roof will deter most cats from walking and sitting on top of the aviary. The lovebirds should not be allowed into the flight when the extra wire is being attached, because they will be frightened by the noise. Actually, a cat on the premises appears to keep the neighbourhood cats out of its territory, and so away from the aviary.

Management of Imported Lovebirds
It is hardly surprising that recently imported lovebirds require more attention than birds bred in captivity. When first acquired, they should be housed in a cage, because this gives them a chance to settle down in their new surroundings. The lovebirds will need to be weaned to a different diet if they are not used to the standard seed mixture, and so as wide a range of food as possible is beneficial at this time, not forgetting the addition of a tonic to their food or water. Soaked millet sprays are always popular, even if hard seed is not readily accepted. Some importers prefer to offer rainwater rather than highly purified, chemically treated tap water which could have an initial adverse effect on newly imported birds. It is perhaps worth boiling tap water before use when the birds have not been in captivity for long.

Imported lovebirds should be purchased preferably in the spring and released into an outside flight with a dry shelter only when the days are warm, and the risk of frost has passed. During the following winter, they may need to be brought inside after the weather turns cold if they show any signs of discomfort, such as fluffing their feathers. Lovebirds are more likely to be adversely affected by exposure to fluctuating temperatures and so they should be kept in a relatively constant temperature.

The flight feathers of imported lovebirds are sometimes cut on one wing. These feathers will be replaced by a new set during the next moult, but when cut, they obviously prevent the bird from flying. In an aviary, such birds can manage easily by climbing along the wire, but if frightened suddenly, they may flap and drop straight on to the floor and injure themselves. Yet nature must be allowed to take its course, and it is not advisable to pull out the cut feathers in a bid to hurry the growth of a new set because of the increased risk of injury and infection to the bird.

Aviary Management
New lovebirds should be released into the shelter of the aviary and confined inside for a couple of days, after being sprayed with a special bird spray which will kill mites and any other external

parasites. They can be shut in simply by sliding the plywood partition across the entrance hole. It is then important to open the ventilation window in the door during the day and partially open the entrance hole at night, so that fresh air can circulate into the shelter. By closing the lovebirds inside, they will find their way around the shelter to the food and water pots.

The best time of day to allow the lovebirds into the outside part of the aviary for their first flight is just before midday. It will not take long for the birds to find the exit, and when they are outside, the food pots in the shelter should be refilled with additional seed. The lovebirds will have eaten before entering the flight, and they should return inside before evening, in search of food. Having put new seed in the pots, and marking the water level, it is possible to see if they have been back inside to feed during the day. Two alternatives will need to be considered if the birds do not return by nightfall. They can either be caught and confined once more in the shelter for a period, or else additional food and water containers may be placed alongside perches in the covered part of the outside flight. However, if the latter course is adopted, the lovebirds will be less inclined to return to the shelter and although this does not matter so much during the summer, they should be encouraged to roost inside in the winter months.

A nestbox must always be available for a pair to sleep in throughout the year. Lovebirds deprived of a nestbox will have to spend the whole night on a perch, and may suffer from frost-bitten toes because of exposure to the cold. In really severe weather, they should be shut inside the shelter at night, and only let out during the daytime. The hen should not lay in the nestbox, when no nesting material is available and if the pair have already reared two rounds of chicks, it is certainly not advisable to allow them to breed again that year. Any eggs should not be removed as they are laid because the hen may just continue laying more and exhaust herself. The eggs can easily be prevented from hatching by making a small hole in the shell with a pin. They should then be returned to the nest, and the hen may continue sitting on them until the end of the incubation period. She will leave the eggs when they fail to hatch and they can be thrown away.

Catching
There comes a time when it will be necessary to catch the

lovebirds either to transfer them to new quarters or examine them. A cloth net is often used for this purpose, but it must be well padded around the edges to prevent the bird being injured by the hard rim. If the net is deep enough, the lovebird could be caught in flight, and then turning the handle to one side should ensure that the bird is retained within the bottom from which it can be removed. The net may alternatively be placed over the lovebird when it is on the wire. Once the bird is safely in the net, it may be transferred directly to a box or cage without handling. Some bird keepers prefer to catch their birds using their hands, maintaining that a net is not as manoeuverable and causes an unnecessary disturbance in the flight. This procedure is not as difficult as it may first appear, but it does require practice so a net is probably the most satisfactory method for a beginner.

Handling

Lovebirds have fairly powerful beaks, and they can draw blood if given the opportunity. Handling any bird is not easy initially, and wearing a pair of thin gloves gives the handler more confidence because there is then little risk of being badly bitten. A right handed person will find it more satisfactory to hold a lovebird in the left hand, which leaves the other hand free to examine the bird as necessary. The head of the lovebird should be grasped firmly between the first and second fingers, but not so firm that the bird is unable to breathe. With its back in the palm of the hand, the lovebird can be restrained by gently clamping the other fingers and thumb around the body. The bird when held in this grip will be unable to bite, and should not struggle very much. Examination is relatively straightforward because most of the body apart from the back is accessible from this position.

Moulting

All birds moult their feathers generally once a year, and these are replaced by a new set. When moulting, lovebirds appear scruffy, and feathers will be seen on the aviary floor. A lovebird in the moult should not be confused with a plucked bird which will be partially bald and may have areas of grey down visible. New feathers develop in sheaths which are occasionally visible as thin spikes amongst the plumage. As their outer covering is removed largely by preening, the feathers open out to form the normal shape. Pet lovebirds kept in the home may drop feathers almost all the year round, but in an outside aviary, few feathers are lost outside the moulting period. A full moult, during which time flight and tail feathers are dropped, may take twelve weeks or more to complete, and lovebirds in a moult are very unlikely to show any interest in breeding. A tonic added to their diet during the moult should help to speed the birds through this debilitating time.

Escapes
The escape of any bird is very disheartening, and thoughts of recapture are clouded by the sense of futility which develops after the accident. However, the lovebird will sometimes return of its own accord to the vicinity of the aviary, particularly if the birds are breeding. It will be difficult to recapture the bird using a net,

*Blue Masked Lovebirds (*Agapornis personata*) perched on a conifer stump.*

because the lovebird will take off again if approached too closely.

A more effective alternative is to place a budgerigar cage filled with seed and water on top of the aviary. The door of the cage is tied and held open by means of a long piece of string extending to a convenient spot beyond the aviary, where it can still be clearly seen. The lovebird should be hungry and will be tempted by a millet spray positioned inside the cage, and so enters cautiously. Once the bird is eating greedily within, the string can be released and then the door swings closed quickly, trapping the escapee. It may be possible to fix the outer door of the aviary in a similar manner, having securely closed the lovebird's mate in the outside flight. Even if the lovebird is not seen, a notice in local shops and papers, as well as contacting other fanciers in the locality may lead to results particularly if someone has already caught the escapee.

The chances of a lovebird surviving away from an aviary are dependent on the immediate environment and the weather. The bird may exist for quite a while providing it has access to food and water. Attempts to establish free-flying lovebirds have not proved successful, but they were first kept at liberty by Charles Buxton on his Surrey estate. Abyssinian Lovebirds bred and lived outside for a winter in the Black Forest after being released. There is a case from several years ago concerning a pair of Masked Lovebirds which escaped from their aviary in Vienna. When one bird was caught, the other returned to the aviary and remained in the neighbourhood for the next month. If an escapee cannot be caught immediately, it may well come back regularly to feed and could be recaptured later. However, it is not recommended to try homing lovebirds because if they get lost they will not be able to fend for themselves in the wild, and so may well meet an unpleasant end.

Chapter 5

Feeding

A balanced diet is the most important part of lovebird management and yet incorrect feeding remains perhaps the most widespread reason for breeding disappointments and underlies many premature deaths. Lovebirds have suffered from being classified as seed eaters. A mixture of seeds certainly forms the basis of their diet in captivity, but a few additional minutes each week spent in preparing green food, fruit and other extras will reap rewards particularly in the breeding season, and also in the bird's condition throughout the year. On a balanced diet, there is an adequate intake of fat, protein and carbohydrate, as well as vitamins, minerals and water to meet the requirements of the body. Deficiencies may have serious effects on the health of a lovebird.

Food Components
Carbohydrates such as starch are used largely by the bird to meet its energy requirements. Fats, as well as being utilised for energy are also stored in the body and used subsequently if the carbohydrate intake falls. Proteins are necessary for the growth and repair of body tissues, ranging from the beak and feathers to muscles. On a seed diet, a carbohydrate deficiency is highly unlikely and since carbohydrate can be converted to fat, the bird should not be short of fat either. Proteins are built up of sub-units known as amino acid residues. The lovebird, however, is unable to manufacture certain of the amino acids, and so these essential amino acids must be present in the food if a deficiency is not to occur.

Few studies have been undertaken with regard to even a budgerigar's dietary requirements, but it is clear that most seeds are deficient in the essential amino acids lysine and methionine.

Methionine is important for feather development while lysine is involved in the pigmentation of feathers. Such deficiencies are most likely to develop when the birds are breeding, because at this time their body resources are taxed to the maximum. Additional protein must then be provided, because in the wild, birds commonly regarded as seed eaters supplement their diet with animal protein in the form of insects. Animal protein is less likely to be deficient in essential amino acids than protein derived from plants.

Vitamins are a diverse group of chemical compounds which have a vital role throughout the body. They cannot be made by the bird and their intake can be increased by using various tonics which are available from pet stores. However, only relatively small quantities of vitamins are required, and indeed an excess will harm the lovebird's health. Minerals such as calcium also form an important part of the bird's diet. They are involved in many body processes, being utilised for example to form the skeleton and the egg shell. Most seeds do not contain a sufficient proportion of minerals. It is therefore necessary to supplement the lovebird's mineral intake and this is commonly achieved by supplying cuttlefish bone and a mineralised grit which also assists digestion. Iodine blocks can be purchased to ensure there is no iodine deficiency. A shortage of minerals will severely handicap breeding results, and hatchability will be low.

Seed

The basic seed mixture for lovebirds consists of plain canary, millet and sunflower seeds. These seeds are imported from various countries, and the quality may vary with each consignment. One of the major regions producing canary seed is North Africa. 'Mazagan' canary seed from the El Jadida area of Morocco is regarded as the most nutritious, but it is also the most expensive. This seed is still often cut and threshed by hand. Australia, Argentina and Canada also export canary seed, and some English seed is advertised from time to time. Many varieties of millet are grown, of which pearl white and plate yellow are widely used. Panicum millet is a favourite with lovebirds, particularly if it is supplied in the form of sprays. The protein content of millet seed is lower than that of canary seed, and it is preferable to offer a mixture of millet seeds. Sunflower seed is rich in oil, and contains amino acids which are not found in sufficient quantities in the cereal seeds.

The number of birds kept will largely determine how the seed is purchased. With only one pair of lovebirds, it is probably most convenient to obtain their requirements from a local shop. However if many are kept, it will pay to buy the seed in larger quantities. Specialist seed firms advertise in most of the avicultural magazines and some pet stores offer reductions on bulk purchases. Canary seed retains its food value for up to five years after harvesting, while sunflower seed remains fresh for about two and a half years providing they are stored correctly.

The condition of the seed is important, and no seed should be bought unless it is clean. When a choice is available, packeted seed ought to be purchased in preference to loose seed, which may have become dusty and so represents a potential hazard to the bird's health. Damp or musty seed is also dangerous to use as bird food. These points must be considered when storing seed. If it is left in a tied plastic sack, condensation may develop and the seed will become damp. Metal containers with a lid are the most satisfactory containers for storage of seed. Moisture is excluded and rodents cannot contaminate the seed with their droppings, which are potentially very harmful to the birds.

The various types of seed can be bought separately and then mixed together. Three parts of canary seed and two of assorted millets form the basis of the mixture, to which a further part of sunflower seed is added. Sunflower seed must be fed relatively sparingly because of its high oil content, since too much fat in the diet will result in liver damage and subsequent death. Either white, black or striped sunflower seed is suitable although some birds show a distinct preference for one variety. The larger grades however should be treated with caution. The food value of seeds is contained in their innermost portion, known as the endosperm, and the outer husk being of no value is discarded by the lovebirds. Large sunflower seed may appear good value, but in some cases, when the seed is cracked open, only a relatively small kernel is contained within. Such seed proves more expensive because a greater part of the seed is being discarded as husk.

Lovebirds take seeds in different quantities during the year. More sunflower seed is likely to be eaten when the weather is cold, and the addition of a small amount of hemp seed to their diet at this time is beneficial. In addition, some lovebirds may prefer canary seed to millet for example, and so not every breeder recommends providing a mixture of these seeds. The birds will simply empty the food pot in search of their favourite seed, scattering the contents everywhere. By providing the seeds in individual containers, the lovebirds can choose what they eat, and waste is reduced.

Grit
Grit is a vital ingredient of a lovebird's diet. When food is swallowed, it enters the crop and can be stored before passing through into the gizzard. Here the grit assists digestion by grinding up the seeds, and prevents the food particles from becoming stuck together. Grit must have rough edges and be of a suitable size for lovebirds if it is to fulfil its functions. The grit container should always be filled regularly even if it is not empty, to ensure an adequate supply is always available to the lovebirds. Addition of a small amount of crushed charcoal to the grit will help to prevent digestive upsets. The grit is gradually dissolved in the acid medium of the gizzard, and provides a useful source of minerals for the bird. Mineralised grit can be supplied on its own, or mixed with oystershell grit. The lovebirds will then benefit from the additional minerals contained in the sea grit.

Cuttlefish Bone
Cuttlefish bone is provided by most fanciers for their lovebirds. As well as containing sodium, it is a major source of calcium, and so is particularly important just before and during the breeding season. Experiments involving domestic chicken hens have revealed that their calcium blood level is doubled when they are in lay, and similar results would doubtless be obtained with lovebirds. A shortage of calcium will result in soft-shelled eggs, thus increasing the risk of egg-binding.

Most seed suppliers stock cuttlefish bone, but it can also be picked up on beaches, especially after a storm. Any loose flesh remaining on the bones should be cut off, and then they can be taken home and boiled. After being cleaned as necessary, the bones are left to soak in water which is changed regularly over several days. They are then dried, preferably in the sun, or else in an oven before being supplied to the birds. Oiled or contaminated

A lightly-marked Yellow and Green Pied Peach-faced Loveb

cuttlefish bones are not worth collecting as they might poison the birds.

Blocks of mortar provide an alternative source of calcium. Crushed hen's egg shells are also sometimes used in addition to cuttlefish, but there is a significant risk of transmitting disease from the chickens to the lovebirds in this way, and cuttlefish bone remains the most satisfactory means of supplying calcium. It should be offered throughout the year, with the soft powdery side accessible to the birds.

Green Food
Green food is a very useful source of nutrients for lovebirds, containing a range of vitamins, proteins and minerals. It helps to correct for the deficiencies which result from an exclusive seed diet. The addition of green food to the diet reduces the risk of fatty degenerative diseases arising from an excessive fat intake. Seeding grasses, chickweed and spinach are the most popular, although lettuce, groundsel, dandelion and plantain will also be accepted by most lovebirds. Individual pairs may show a preference for a certain plant. It is essential that any green food fed is absolutely fresh, because otherwise complaints such as enteritis will ensue. Frosted green food should not be supplied and if in doubt about a particular plant it is advisable not to feed it, in case it is harmful to the birds.

With chemical spraying being so widespread today, care must be taken to ensure that all green food fed is uncontaminated and it should always be washed before feeding. Plants growing on roadside verges are particularly dangerous. Apart from the risk of being sprayed, they will probably contain a relatively higher content of lead, derived from engine fumes. This compound can be retained within the body until toxic levels are accumulated.

The safest source of green food is that which has been grown at home. Providing there is a space in the garden for a row of spinach beet, this plant can be easily grown from seed, and will provide a regular supply of green food throughout most of the year. Without a garden, it is still possible to ensure that only uncontaminated green food is available for the lovebirds. A container such as a clean plastic margarine tub can be lined with wet tissues, and then plain canary seed is sprinkled on top. The seed germinates and, depending on the temperature, fresh green shoots soon develop if the tissues are kept moist. This grass can then be cut and fed to the birds. Dried spinach and other green foods are sold in most pet stores, but these are rarely accepted with the relish shown by birds for fresh greens.

Green food should be fed in small quantities regularly, rather than a large amount given at odd intervals since this will disturb the digestive processes. The amount of green food needs to be increased when there are chicks in the nest, but some breeders will only feed it early in the day. This ensures that the parents must fill their offsprings' crops with seed, which is more substantial than green food, at dusk. Imported lovebirds will not often take to green food immediately, but if it is offered regularly, then they will try it to satisfy their curiosity. Some lovebirds also appreciate fruit such as apple, while carrot is popular with others.

Soaked Seed

As seed begins to germinate, changes occur in the food stores of the endosperm. The protein content increases and B group vitamin levels rise, so that soaked seed is a useful addition to the diet especially at breeding time. Soaking stimulates germination, and soaked plain canary seed and oats are often supplied to lovebirds.

The seed is washed under a tap in a sieve, and then left in water in a bowl for about a day. It should be rinsed and drained thoroughly before being fed to the birds. Although the full advantages of soaked seed cannot be realised for about four days, it is safer to feed the seed after it has been soaked for only a day or so, rather than leaving it until shoots develop. There is a distinct risk particularly in hot weather of harmful moulds and bacteria growing on the seed, which will then smell unpleasant. For the same reason, soaked seed cannot be left for long in the aviary if it is not all eaten, and so no more than will be consumed in a day should be provided. Soaked oats are very fattening and must be fed sparingly, while soaked millet sprays are a popular rearing food.

Cod Liver Oil

Cod liver oil is a useful supplementary source of vitamin D_3 and is conveniently mixed in with seed. Vitamin D_3 is usually made by ultra violet light falling on the bird's feathers and skin, and is very important in controlling the calcium levels of the body. Cod liver oil is therefore particularly valuable for lovebirds kept inside without access to sunlight, because they are most likely to suffer from a vitamin D deficiency.

A limited quantity of millet and canary seed mixed with cod liver oil can be given about two or three times a week. The correct ratio is one teaspoonful of oil per pound (340 gms) of seed. The oil can be tipped on top of the seed in a bowl and left to percolate down to the bottom. Stirring with a spoon will ensure that the concoction is thoroughly mixed. It is advisable to prepare the mixture as required because the cod liver oil may turn rancid. Rancid or excess cod liver oil will cause a vitamin E deficiency, which is normally rare because most seeds contain sufficient quantities of this vitamin.

Prepared Tonics
An artificial tonic should not be necessary if the bird is on a well-balanced diet which includes green food. However, when a lovebird is recovering from illness or during breeding, and especially with newly imported stock, a tonic will be useful. Special tonics prepared for birds are sold in pet shops. 'Abidec' which is a popular choice is only available from chemists and contains a wide range of vitamins and is marketed primarily for human babies. It should be bought from a chemist who has a fairly rapid turnover of stock because it has an expiry date after which it cannot be used. One drop of 'Abidec' given in water about twice a week is sufficient for lovebirds. A yeast-based powder such as 'P.Y.M.' sprinkled on the seed is a valuable source of trace minerals as well as B series vitamins. It is most important to follow the instructions when using tonics because, as mentioned earlier, an overdose of vitamins may be positively harmful to the bird.

Other Food Additives for Imported and Breeding Lovebirds
Although it is not a commercially prepared tonic, milk given in a 50:50 ratio with the lovebird's water regularly will ensure that there is no deficiency of the essential amino acid lysine, which is most likely to develop during the breeding season. In hot weather, the milk is likely to go off quickly and will need to be changed perhaps twice a day. The water containers must be thoroughly washed after giving milk, and this also applies to all pots used for soft food. Nectar sold for hummingbirds provides a readily

available source of energy when diluted as suggested with water, and is particularly beneficial to newly imported lovebirds. This mixture should not be offered in an open pot and will have to be mixed fresh perhaps twice daily.

There is a wide range of soft foods available today, although bread and milk is still regarded in some quarters as an adequate rearing food. Egg food sold for canaries may be accepted by some breeding pairs as will the balanced cereal diet marketed as 'Farex'. Both need to be moistened with water before use. High protein budgerigar or insectivorous soft food are other possible alternatives which are suitable for lovebirds. If these foods are ignored, then it may be possible to encourage the parents to sample them by placing green food on top of the mixture. The lovebirds might inadvertently eat some soft food with the green food and then develop a taste for it. Some pairs will accept a few mealworms given daily.

Feeding Utensils
No standard seed hoppers are produced commercially for lovebirds, and those sold for budgerigars are unsuitable. It may be possible to make a satisfactory hopper, but it will need to be of metal and must not jam with a mixture which contains relatively large sunflower seed. Yet even after overcoming these difficulties, there is no guarantee that the lovebirds will put their heads in through hopper holes to eat the seed.

Open food pots are generally used for feeding lovebirds. The containers should be made either of china, metal or tough plastic because otherwise they may be chewed up and destroyed. The actual positioning of the food pots will depend largely on the birds, although it is sensible to have the seed protected under cover, preferably in the shelter. Some lovebirds refuse to eat from pots on the floor, and so the containers must hook on to the aviary wire. The birds will not have to alight directly on to the sides of the container if it is located near a perch, and this helps to reduce unnecessary seed scattering. When the pots are on the floor of the shelter less seed is wasted, but neither food nor water containers should be positioned underneath perches, because they will be fouled by droppings. Cuttlefish bone can either be wired to the aviary mesh, or attached by a special clip. Grit is best provided in an open pot, since there is no risk of the flow being interrupted as may happen if a closed container is used.

There are a variety of water vessels on the market. A chicken-type drinker with an inverted jam jar on the floor ensures a regular supply. The plastic water containers sold for cages are suitable for lovebirds in aviaries. These come complete with a clip so they can be attached to the aviary wire without difficulty. Tinted green 'Oasis' water bottles ensure the water within remains fresh for up to three days, and the tinting reduces the growth of algae. They are graduated so that the volume of water drunk each day can be noted. It is worth double checking the flow of water through the bottles after filling them, by tapping the bottle gently on the back. Water should emerge through the spout, but if they are filled incorrectly water will continue dripping on to the floor. The water containers should be positioned in a cool part of the aviary, particularly if the water is mixed with anything else such as a tonic or milk.

Analysis of the Ingredients of Foodstuffs used for Lovebirds

Food	Carbo-hydrate	Fat	Protein	Mineral
Canary seed	55	4	17	3
Millet	56	5	14	3
Sunflower	22	21	14	3
Hemp	25	30	16	6
Milk	—	0·5	10	1
Apple	15	—	0·5	0·5
Carrot	10	0·1	1·0	1
Dandelion	11	1	2·5	1
Lettuce	2	0·1	1	1
Whole egg	—	16·5	12·5	1·5

The percentages expressed above are a useful guide, but may vary according to the condition and age of the foodstuff provided. Water is the other major constituent of these foods.

Chapter 6

Breeding

Some lovebirds will breed throughout the year, but the breeding season should be restricted to the warmer months between April and late September. The chances of success will be much greater at this time of year. There is less risk of the hens becoming egg-bound and the eggs once laid will not chill so quickly because of the higher temperatures. More daylight ensures that the parents will have longer to feed their chicks.

Lovebirds however require a nestbox for roosting in throughout the year, and so it may not be very easy to dissuade an eager hen from laying at an unusual time of year. Separation of the sexes is rarely practical, but the nestbox can be replaced after the breeding season with another containing only peat. The breeding stimulus will then be reduced if no nesting material is available. Some species breed more readily in captivity than others. The Red-faced Lovebird has only been bred on a very few occasions, but Peach-faced, Fischer's and Masked Lovebirds reproduce quite readily, and home-bred stock is often advertised, although it is not easy to recognise true pairs.

Sexing
Sexing lovebirds correctly is a problem especially encountered with the more readily available species. Those which are sexually dimorphic as described earlier are the Madagascar, Red-faced and Abyssinian, and so pairs can be recognised easily by the differences in plumage between the sexes. The pelvic bone test is useful for sexing other lovebirds, but it is only reliable when they are in breeding condition. This test is simple to carry out once the bird has been caught, because the two prominent pelvic bones can then be located between the legs above the vent. If there is only a narrow space between them, the chances are that the bird

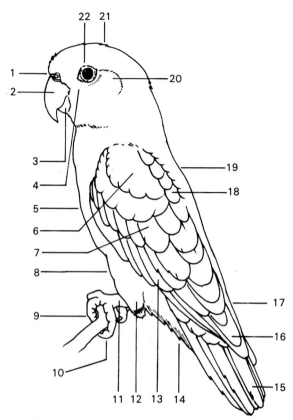

Glossary of terms

1 Care
2 Upper mandible
3 Lower mandible
4 Lores
5 Breast
6 Lesser wing coverts
7 Secondary coverts
8 Abdomen
9 Toes
10 Claw
11 Shank

12 Thigh
13 Secondaries
14 Under tail coverts
15 Central tail feathers
16 Primaries
17 Rump
18 Scapulars
19 Mantle
20 Ear coverts
21 Occiput (crown)
22 Periophthalmic (eye) ring

is a cock. In the case of a hen in breeding condition, the bones are more pliable, and the gap is larger being about a quarter of an inch (6 mm) in diameter, which allows for the passage of eggs. The value of this technique is limited however, because it is not reliable for immature birds, and when not laying, a mature hen has a reduced gap between the bones.

The size of a lovebird is not a satisfactory indication of its sex, because not only are genetic and nutritional factors involved, but also birds found in different parts of their range will probably show a natural size variation. It is generally accepted however that all hens have flatter broader skulls than cock birds. Earlier theories that cock Black-cheeked and Nyasa Lovebirds could be recognised by their darker reddish-brown irides have been refuted, since further observations have revealed that the eye colour of both sexes changes as the bird gets older. The suggestion that cock Black-cheeked Lovebirds have more yellow on their inner wing-coverts than females may be equally suspect, because scattered yellow areas of plumage are not uncommon on parrot-like birds, probably resulting from a dietary deficiency.

The behaviour of two lovebirds housed together provides more useful clues to their sex. When mating is seen taking place, it can be assumed that the birds are a true pair, but if the advances of one bird are constantly rejected, then the lovebirds are probably two cocks. This will be confirmed if the birds only roost in the nestbox, and no eggs are forthcoming during the year. If a large number of infertile eggs are laid, it is probable that two hens ere being kept together, particularly when they spend time in the nestbox during the day.

A recent technique, known as faecal steroid analysis, can accurately determine a bird's sex by testing for the sex hormones present in its droppings. Although this test is not yet commercially available in Britain, it may prove particularly valuable for determining the sex of the more expensive lovebird mutations, and so will increase the likelihood of breeding success. However for the moment, the only sure way for a pair to be distinguished is for them to nest and rear youngsters. If space and finances permit, it is worth purchasing several lovebirds, and allowing the birds to choose their own mates while keeping a close watch to prevent possible fighting. A pair of lovebirds will go to roost together in a box at dusk, and then they can be distinguished from

BREEDING REGISTER

PAIR No. .... COCK .... HEN ....

Date	Date due to Hatch	Number of eggs	Number of young	Remarks	Description of Young, with Ring Numbers or distinguishing marks (if any)

PAIR No. .... COCK .... HEN ....

The pair number will be entered from the label on the breeding cage or aviary, together with the name, or number, of the cock and hen (obtained from the Pedigree Register). Due to Hatch indicates the twenty-third day from the date the first egg was laid. Remarks: Under this heading infertile or broken eggs, dead or plucked chicks, etc., should be recorded.

the remainder of the flock. Once recognized, a pair should be moved to separate accommodation.

Nest Boxes
Most lovebirds are not very fussy about nesting receptacles and artificial boxes made of wood are now usually provided. In the past, hollow tree trunk logs were popular, but these are harder to find today, and access to the nest is not always as easy as when a well-designed box is used; they are however preferred by imported birds and have a more natural appearance. Red-faced Lovebirds will probably ignore a typical nestbox, because in the wild they breed in termites' nests. Attempts to recreate more natural conditions for these birds are discussed in the section devoted to this species. With the exception of the rare Mount Apo Lorikeet and the Hanging Parrots, lovebirds are the only parrot-like birds which use nesting material, and so the dimensions of the box need to be relatively larger. A nestbox about 8 inches (20 cm) wide, 9 inches (23 cm) high and 6 inches (15 cm) deep with an entrance hole 2 inches (5 cm) in diameter will be adequate for all common species of lovebirds. If the entrance hole is any larger, too much light will be admitted and the birds may ignore the box.

A piece of dowel about 3 inches (76 mm) in length should be positioned just below the entrance so that the lovebirds can perch outside before going in or out of the box. It is convenient to have a hinged roof on the nest box because in this position, no chicks are likely to fall out on the floor when the box is inspected, as they could if one of the sides opened. As well as hinging the roof, it is a good idea to fasten it by a solid metal catch, which ensures that the lid is not opened accidentally by the birds or blown up by the wind.

Timber or plywood at least 1 inch (25 mm) thick is ideal for constructing nestboxes. Wood of this thickness will not only stand up to the onslaught of the lovebird's beaks, but it should also help to keep the interior at a more constant temperature, which is necessary if hatching is to be successful. Lovebirds have a reputation for producing a high proportion of chicks which do not hatch, and are referred to as being dead-in-the-shell. One of the possible causes of this problem is low humidity, and so as a further refinement, particularly if the birds are kept indoors, a

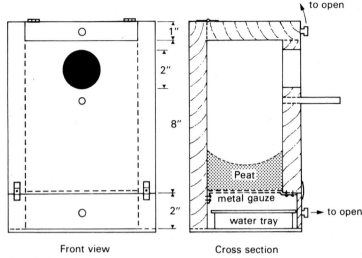

Front view   Cross section

A typical nestbox.

shallow tray of water should be placed in a separate compartment under a false floor in the nestbox. This intermediate floor is constructed using a fine but substantial metal gauze because there is a danger that as the chicks increase in weight, the floor may collapse into the water tray. The gauze must therefore be firmly attached to the walls of the nestbox, and any rough edges can be bent underneath into the lower compartment which is inaccessible to the birds. The water tray will only need to be refilled perhaps once or twice during the incubation period.

The false bottom of the nestbox can be covered with damp peat, which helps to ensure there is a relatively high degree of humidity within the box. The lovebirds will then build their nest on top of the peat. The nestbox during the breeding season is better located in the outside flight, where the humidity will be relatively higher than in the shelter. It can be right outside in the open, provided the roof of the box is a tight fit, because otherwise in a summer downpour the interior may become absolutely saturated. Once the chicks are wet, they rapidly lose heat, and will soon die if their parents leave the nest for long. Passing cats are more likely to disturb the adults if the nestbox is in the uncovered part of the flight. Wood or brackets securely attached to the nestbox can be easily screwed on to a suitable part of the aviary structure, preferably in a relatively cool but protected position. The box itself should be fixed as high as possible, bearing in mind that the roof must be free to open so the inside can be inspected.

Nesting Material
Lovebirds will soon strip the bark off the perches in their aviary, and additional smaller branches from non-poisonous trees such as willow should be provided during the breeding season. Once the bark is removed, it is then carried to the nestbox, either in the beak or rather quaintly tucked under the feathers depending on the species. Madagascar, Red-faced and Abyssinian Lovebirds carry many small strips placed between feathers throughout the body, while Peach-faced Lovebirds build their nest from larger pieces of material transported in the region of the lower back and rump. The females of all species are generally responsible for nest construction, and the hen Abyssinian Lovebird is unique in utilising some of her feathers as nesting material. Some pairs will add old millet sprays and green food to the nest, if kept short of suitable material. During the breeding season, the nest should be left undisturbed after the first round of chicks, and more nesting material may be appreciated before a second clutch of eggs is laid. Fresh green bark helps to increase the humidity within the nestbox.

Breeding Introduction
Lovebirds should not be encouraged to breed until they are at least a year old, although cocks may be fertile when only five months old. When they are fully developed their body resources can be devoted entirely to rearing healthy chicks, but while the birds are still growing the chances are that the growth of both the young parents themselves and their chicks will be stunted.

If the lovebirds have been kept inside for the winter, it is unlikely that they will nest until the middle of the summer and only one round of chicks can be expected. Imported birds will probably not breed at all during their first year, because of the drastic change in their environment, but captive-bred lovebirds purchased in the autumn will usually reproduce in the following year. Lovebirds will only breed if they are in good condition, and used to their surroundings.

Concerning Eggs and Chicks
When she is about to lay, the hen will enter the box more regularly and spend longer periods inside. More cuttlefish will be consumed, and the hen's droppings may be noticeably looser and change slightly in colour. The birds will mate at this time, and only one successful mating is required to fertilise a clutch of eggs.

The hen will not necessarily sit tight as soon as the first egg is laid. This behaviour is quite normal, and, since the white eggs are laid on alternate days, it helps to ensure that the chicks hatch closer together. Four to six eggs are about the usual number laid in a clutch. The cock does not assist in incubating the eggs, but will enter the nestbox and feed his mate, as well as roosting alongside her at night. There is no need to disturb the lovebirds after they have gone to nest, but if the hen is seen off the nest towards the middle of the estimated incubation period, it should not harm to glance quickly into the box. It is then possible to check the number of eggs laid and perhaps top up the water level in the tray at the base of the nestbox. The hen should return to the box without problems, but one's curiosity must be restrained if the weather is cold, because the eggs will soon be chilled so the hen must only be off them for a very short time. Indeed throughout the breeding season, the birds ought to be left alone as much as possible unless one of the pair shows signs of distress.

The incubation period for all species is about twenty-three days, although the exact time may vary according to when incubation began. The nest should not be inspected again until at least a week after the last egg was due to hatch. With any luck, there will be some chicks visible and those which are at least seven days old will have their eyes open. However if none of the eggs have hatched by this time, they should be removed so that the adults will probably go to nest again almost immediately. When the eggs are examined in a good light, if they appear clear then mating was not successful. On the other hand, particularly if the shell is opaque and discoloured, an embryo may have developed inside but failed to hatch for one reason or another. This can be confirmed by carefully removing part of the surrounding shell.

*A young close-rung Blue Peach-faced Lovebird (*Agapornis roseicollis*). The beak colour soon lightens once the bird has left the nest.*

With a nest full of hungry mouths, the lovebirds will require more food and water, and it is wise to offer some of the beneficial extras mentioned in the feeding section. A selection should be supplied even before the eggs have been laid, because correct feeding plays an important part in bringing birds into top breeding condition. Lovebird chicks grow rapidly and some may leave the nest when they are only six weeks old, although seven to eight weeks is more usual. If they emerge from the nest too soon, the young lovebirds may not be able to fly very strongly. They will cling and climb on the aviary wire, and at this time are particularly exposed to attacks from cats, or other lovebirds in adjoining enclosures if there is inadequate double wiring. The youngsters generally find their own way back to the nestbox which they share with the adults, but if a young bird remains on the floor of the aviary just before dusk falls, it should be returned to the nest. This is particularly important if the chicks have been plucked, because they are then deprived of the natural insulation provided by their feathers, and so get cold very quickly.

The young lovebirds are fed largely by the cock for about a further fortnight or so after leaving the nest. The youngsters should then be removed as soon as they are eating independently, or if their parents show signs of attacking them. There are few sights more disheartening having bred lovebirds successfully than finding the offspring mutilated or killed by the adults, and in this respect Peach-faced Lovebirds in particular have gained a murderous reputation.

Ringing

Fanciers are somewhat divided over the merits of ringing lovebirds. Split or closed rings can be used, each of which have advantages and disadvantages over the other type. The closed ring, as the description suggests, is a continuous circular band which can only be applied at a specific age when the lovebird is still in the nest. Such birds are advertised with the initials C.R. and the ring will carry the year of issue and probably an identification number and the breeder's initials. A closed-ring lovebird has therefore been bred in captivity. The split ring can be applied at any age, and is a useful identification marker, although it does not act as a reliable age guide.

Bird rings of a suitable size for lovebirds may be ordered from one of the firms who advertise in the magazine *Cage and Aviary Birds*. When ordering the rings it is important to state that they are for lovebirds because there are many sizes produced. Plastic rings are unsuitable because they can be chewed off by the lovebirds and although only closed metal rings are usually advertised, most firms will split them for an additional small charge. Closed rings for lovebirds must be applied when the

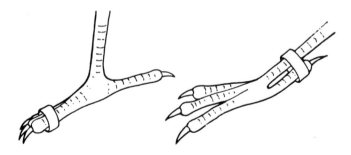

The correct way to ring a young bird with a closed ring.

chicks are five or six days old. If the bird is too young, the ring will either slip off or fix itself higher up the leg than is intended, and the limb may be damaged as a result. When the chick is older, the ring is too small to pass over the feet.

Hints on how to ring lovebirds are usually supplied with the rings. A right-handed person will find it more convenient to hold the chick in the left hand. The three longest toes of one leg are gathered together and the ring placed in position so that it encloses them. It can then be slid backwards over these toes up the leg. The ring is passed over the remaining fourth toe, which is thus kept parallel with the leg using either a ringing tool or matchstick. Once the fourth toe is free the procedure is complete and the ring should slide easily up and down this part of the leg. Split rings can be opened and applied directly to the leg, even after the chick has left the nest. Care must be taken however to ensure that the split ends of the ring make a tight fit together around the leg, because otherwise the lovebird may get caught up by the ring in the aviary and injure itself.

Breeding Problems

Very few breeders can claim that they have breeding seasons completely free from problems year after year, particularly if several pairs are kept. However, even in a bad season some chicks will be reared, but when the results are consistently bad it suggests that there may be a fault either in the stock or its management. The lovebirds cannot be expected to breed successfully unless they are a pair in breeding condition. A common cause for lack of success with the more readily available species is that two cocks are housed together under the guise of a pair and so not surprisingly, no eggs are forthcoming. An exchange of one of the birds with another breeder may effect an answer to this problem.

Egg binding is especially likely to occur if the lovebirds start breeding early in the year before the weather is warm. Chilling depresses the muscular activity which is necessary for expulsion of the eggs, and the egg is therefore retained within the body and causes a blockage. Budgerigar breeders offer seed mixed with cod liver oil to reduce the risk of egg binding under these circumstances. Mis-shapen or enlarged eggs may result in egg binding, and suggest that the hen may be reaching the end of her reproductive life, particularly if earlier clutches have consisted of only a relatively few eggs. The risk of soft-shelled eggs and subsequent egg binding should be eliminated by providing an adequate supply of cuttlefish bone. The treatment for egg binding can be found in the chapter dealing with accidents and ailments.

A clutch of clear eggs indicates that they were not fertilised by the cock. There are several possible reasons, and if all the eggs are clear after two or three rounds, then the pair should be split up and another cock introduced to the hen. It may be that the hen stayed in the nestbox too long so mating did not take place, but it is more likely that the supposed cock is another hen, or else is too old to breed successfully.

If there are dead chicks within the eggs it is probable that the humidity was too low for successful hatching. Alternatively, the chicks may have been too weak to free themselves from the egg shell, which suggests the stock is lacking in stamina and could be too closely related. The humidity level can be monitored by purchasing a hygrometer from a hardware store, and positioning it in the vicinity of the nesting box. Some suggestions to ensure a high degree of humidity have been mentioned already. Pairs breeding inside are particularly likely to produce a high percentage of chicks which are dead in the shell, and so it is useful to soak the nestbox in water before attaching it back in position on the cage. It can then be sprayed from the outside at intervals. Most lovebirds will roll about on damp green food and this helps to increase the humidity in the box. A shallow bath provided on the floor enables the hen to bathe and then she returns to the nest with her feathers wet.

Fostering
When an injury or accident befalls one of the pair, the remaining lovebird may well continue to rear the chicks, although if the hen dies the chances of success are reduced and any eggs will be ignored by the cock. Eggs can be fostered safely to another pair who laid at a similar time, but no pair should be expected to hatch more than seven eggs. If the transferred eggs are marked gently with a felt-tip pen, it is possible to discover later whether or not they were hatched successfully.

Under certain circumstances therefore it will be necessary to remove young lovebirds if they are to survive. Most pairs make good foster parents and will accept chicks of the same group without problems. The young must be transferred to a nest containing chicks of a compatible age, otherwise it is likely that the youngest will not be reared successfully. Young chicks which appear dead may revive if they are held in the hand for a few minutes. When signs of life return, they can then be placed in another nest. Hens however rarely desert a nest unless they have been frightened, and if possible the reason for the disturbance should be found. At night, animals, car or other lights flashing in the vicinity of the box can disturb the parents who then leave the nestbox. The eggs or chicks become cold and are lifeless by the morning.

Hand rearing requires both time and dedication, but if no other foster parents are available, there is little choice in the matter. Success will be far more likely if the chicks have their eyes open and are beginning to feather up. The young birds should be placed in a small box lined with tissues, and kept in an even temperature of about 85°F (29°C), such as an airing cupboard or a hospital cage, failing access to an incubator which is suitable for use as a brooder. The maxim for successful hand feeding is a little food given often, on demand. A soft food such as 'Farex' makes an ideal rearing food, and needs to be mixed with milk and water as well as a vitamin and mineral supplement.

The food is best given to the chick on the end of a spoon with a small amount at a time being placed in the bird's mouth. If too much is given at once, there is an increased risk of choking the chick. A syringe is easier to manipulate, but its nozzle will probably be too thin to dispense the feeding mixture. With only a few feathers on the body, the crop can be seen at the base of the neck, and when it fills up to a reasonable size, the lovebird has been fed sufficiently. If the crop is full of air, this must be gently squeezed out by hand rather than being pricked with a pin. The frequency of feeding will depend on the age of the chick, but at no time should the crop be allowed to empty. When one chick in a nest looks poorly, it can be removed and fed by hand as a last resort. After being returned to the others, it will hopefully receive its full ration from then onwards. However, adult lovebirds rarely seem to rear a chick which is slightly sickly or develops slower than the rest, as it probably has an inherited weakness. When the lovebirds are nearly fully feathered, seeds should be introduced to their diet and they can be gradually weaned off the soft food.

*Black-masked Lovebird (*Agapornis personata*). An ideal species for the novice owner.*

Plucking

Some adult lovebirds appear to delight in removing feathers from themselves or their youngsters which then emerge partially or wholly bald from the nest. The causes for this behaviour are likely to reside in their diet, or may result from boredom, indeed love-birds kept in cages are particularly susceptible to this vice. The metabolism of fat generates more heat than that of carbohydrate and an excess of fat, in the form of sunflower seed for example, may be a contributory factor to feather plucking. For this reason, if hemp seed is fed, it must only be supplied very sparingly even in cold winters. It has been shown that this complaint is inherited in some cases, although the feathers of all plucked chicks will regrow in time. Access to bathing facilities may reduce the risk of plucking when lovebirds are kept inside.

Chapter 7

Genetics and the Colour Mutations

Gregor Mendel was the first person to investigate the science of heredity, which has become known as genetics. Using the data obtained from his experiments with sweet pea plants, Mendel was able to produce a set of laws governing the transmission of characters from one generation to the next. These laws have enabled the breeder of colour lovebirds to accurately predict which pairing should yield the highest number of mutation offspring.

All the characters of an organism, including its sex, are controlled by genes located on minute structures called chromosomes which are found in every cell of the body. Chromosomes occur in pairs, which are usually of the same length except for a pair of sex chromosomes. In a cock bird, the sex chromosomes referred to as XX are of an equal length, while in the hen, these chromosomes are known as XY with the X chromosome being longer than the Y form. It is interesting that the situation is reversed in man and other mammals, with a male possessing XY chromosomes. The Y character is concerned only with determining the bird's sex and appears to have little other significance. The X chromosome is important for the transmission of certain colours, which are referred to as sex-linked. This is because the genes for these colours are carried on the X component of the sex chromosomes for birds of either sex.

Mutations
A mutation may always occur when the sperm from the male fertilises the female ovum, which then develops to form the egg. If any of the chromosomes are altered even slightly at this time,

then a mutation such as a change in colour will be inevitable in the chick. Every embryo receives only one set of chromosomes from each parent, and these are paired to form the usual number.

The colour of all birds is largely determined by the relative proportions of the colouring pigments in the feathers. There are two groups of such pigments which have been identified in lovebirds, and both are in fact widespread throughout the animal kingdom. The carotenoids are responsible for red and yellow coloration, while the presence of the indole derivative melanin produces a black appearance of which blue is a component. If there is a shortage or relative excess of one or more of these pigments, then a change in the colour of the bird will result, and this is known technically as heterochrosis.

In parrot-like birds, melanin is most commonly affected and so areas of blue and black plumage are correspondingly modified. Green, as all artists know, can be made from a mixture of blue and yellow paints so basically when blue is completely absent from the feathers, areas which are normally blue appear white, and green areas will be yellow. Any black coloration will be similarly altered. Red feathering remains unchanged if the carotenoid pigments are not affected.

Lutino Lovebirds such as the very rare Red-faced and the Nyasa thus retain their red faces, but they could be distinguished from a yellow form by virtue of their red eyes and because areas of blue such as the rump of the Red-faced appear white. In a yellow lovebird most but not all of the melanin pigment is absent and this is known as panthochromism. Hence in the Golden Cherry Peach-faced, the rump is not white but a pale blue and the eyes remain black. Both the melanin and carotenoid pigments are absent in an albino lovebird so that the red colour of the eyes results only from the circulation of blood. In the white or silver form, some pigment remains so the eyes are dark as in a normal.

Cyanthinism occurs when the carotenoid pigments do not develop in the feathers. Blue plumage then replaces green, and where yellow is normally found on its own, only white feathering is seen. Black is unaffected however, and this change underlies the appearance of the Blue Masked Lovebird. When some but not all of the carotenoid pigments are absent, then a Pastel Blue Lovebird results. The Peach-faced mutation of this type for example still possesses a reddish face with a body colour which has a more greenish appearance than a genuine blue lovebird. The situation appears to be reversed in the Jade Peach-faced which lacks a similar amount of melanin, and so is perhaps best known as the Pastel Light Green. In this case, the body colour lies between yellow and green.

Pied lovebirds show uneven areas of yellow and green plumage. The mutation occurred spontaneously, and results from the absence of melanin in the yellow regions. Pastel Blue Pied Peach-faced Lovebirds were then bred and these have their pastel colour interrupted with areas of a yellow tinge, because some carotenoid pigment remains. When the carotenoids are completely absent a Blue and White Pied can be expected.

A cinnamon lovebird has its black coloration diluted so that areas of brown occur where there are naturally black markings. A true cinnamon has red eyes which are especially prominent in a young bird. This is a rare mutation at present, although a form may occur to some extent in the wild because the heads of Black-masked Lovebirds vary in colour from a normal black to dark brown. This species also shows more variation in its overall coloration than do other lovebirds.

Colour Inheritance
Most of the common mutations now available have proved to be recessive in their mode of inheritance. Furthermore, the blue, pastel blue, yellow and white forms have proved to be of a straightforward recessive type. This means that a normal lovebird is always dominant when paired to a blue lovebird for example, and so all the youngsters resulting from this pairing will appear normal. The external appearance of a bird is described as its phenotype, distinguishing it from its genetic make-up or genotype which may well be different, as in this case. Although the chicks have a normal phenotype, they all carry the blue factor as part of their genotype, and so are regarded as being split for blue. Split birds are revealed by the symbol / in the table below, and normal is written first because this is the dominant character. The blue colour will emerge if these splits are paired to visible blue lovebirds or to similar splits.

Colour expectancies for recessive mutations, using blue as an example:

1. Blue × normal ⟶ 100% normal/blue.
2. Blue × normal/blue ⟶ 50% blue + 50% normal/blue.
3. Blue × blue ⟶ 100% blue.
4. Normal/blue × normal ⟶ 50% normal/blue + 50% normal.
5. Normal/blue × normal/blue ⟶ 50% normal/blue + 25% normal + 25% blue.

The rare Lutino Nyasa mutation is also an autosomal recessive, like the above, but the Lutino Peach-faced has a different mode of inheritance.

Pied Lovebirds
It is now thought that there are two forms of the pied mutation, as in budgerigars. One type is recessive, and its mode of inheritance is identical to the blue form listed above. This means that when a recessive pied is paired to a normal, there are no pied offspring although all the resulting lovebirds will be split for pied.

The dominant form can be distinguished because a similar pairing with a normal should yield a proportion of pied lovebirds. This pied character, being dominant would be present as either a single or double factor, and hence determines the relative proportions of dominant pieds in any nest. There are five possible pairings for Pied Peach-faced Lovebirds:

1. Dominant Pied (double factor) × Dominant Pied (double factor) ⟶ 100% Dominant Pied (double factor).
2. Dominant Pied (single factor) × Dominant Pied (single factor) ⟶ 50% Dominant Pied (single factor) + 25% Dominant Pied (double factor) + 25% normal.
3. Dominant Pied (single factor) × Dominant Pied (double factor) ⟶ 50% Dominant Pied (single factor) + 50% Dominant Pied (double factor).
4. Dominant Pied (double factor) × normal ⟶ 100% Dominant Pied (single factor).
5. Dominant Pied (single factor) × normal ⟶ 50% Dominant Pied (single factor) + 50% normal.

It is likely that most dominant pieds available will be single factor birds, since normal lovebirds will have been used to develop the mutation. By pairing such pieds together or with known double factor birds a strain of double factor pied lovebirds could be built up, but experimental pairings will be necessary initially to separate these from single factor birds in the same nest.

Sex-Linked Recessive Mutations

The inheritance of Lutino in the Peach-faced is more complex, because although this mutation is recessive it is also linked specifically to the X component of the sex chromosomes. The expectancies for the sex-linked mutations are given below, and albino and cinnamon characters may well prove identical.

1. Normal cock $\times$ lutino hen $\longrightarrow$ 50% normal/lutino cocks + 50% normal hens

2. Normal/lutino cock $\times$ normal hen $\longrightarrow$ 25% normal cocks + 25% normal/lutino cocks + 25% normal hens + 25% lutino hens

3. Normal/lutino cock $\times$ lutino hen $\longrightarrow$ 25% normal/lutino cocks + 25% lutino cocks + 25% normal hens + 25% lutino hens

4. Lutino cock $\times$ normal hen $\longrightarrow$ 50% normal/lutino cocks + 50% lutino hens

5. Lutino cock $\times$ lutino hen $\longrightarrow$ 100% lutino cocks and hens

A hen cannot be split for a sex-linked mutation such as lutino, because she has only one X sex chromosome. If the lutino factor is present, it must be attached to this chromosome, while there is no corresponding portion on the shorter Y chromosome which could repress the colour. A cock bird however has paired X sex chromosomes, and with two such chromosomes present, it is possible for the normal factor on one to be dominant over a recessive which is carried on the other. The non sex-linked Lutino Nyasa Lovebird mutation emerged relatively early, as happened during the development of the lutino budgerigar. Both this and an identical albino mutation were however lost in the case of the budgerigar. Hens of this type could be split for the colour concerned.

All the figures given in this chapter are based on the expected results from a large number of matings. In any one round it is unlikely that the results will be necessarily in the proportions given, apart from pairings which yield 100% of one colour, but even then there may be more cocks than hens or vice-versa. If no lutino chicks result from the pairing of a supposedly split cock to a lutino hen, this does not mean that the cock has a normal genotype, because such a decision would need to be based on the colours of the chicks obtained over several rounds. One lutino chick from these birds will confirm that the cock is split for lutino. The same reasoning applies to all pairings involving mutations, since their occurrence is determined solely by chance. On the other hand, all lutinos may be bred in one nest, and this would only be expected if both parents were themselves lutinos.

Olive Peach-faced

The breeding of the Olive Peach-faced Lovebird is potentially the most important breakthrough in the search for new colours. It appears to correspond to the dark mutation of the budgerigar which was first bred in 1915. This lovebird mutation is still rare, and steps must be taken to preserve its existence. Its mode of inheritance is somewhat different from the sports previously described, since it shows incomplete dominance when paired to a normal. The Olive Peach-faced is a double dark factor bird and when it is mated with a normal, Jade Peach-faced Lovebirds all of which possess a single dark factor, are bred. Hence the Jade is lighter than the Olive mutation. On the continent, a mutation which appears to be identical to the Jade is variously known as the Greywing or Pastel Light Green lovebird. The expected results from pairings involving the dark factor are:

1. Olive (double factor) × normal ⟶ 100% Jade (single factor).

2. Olive (double factor) × Jade (single factor) ⟶ 50% Olive (double factor) + 50% Jade (single factor).

3. Olive (double factor) × Olive (double factor) ⟶ 100% Olive (double factor).

4. Jade (single factor) × normal ⟶ 50% Jade (single factor) + 50% normal.

5. Jade (single factor) × Jade (single factor) ⟶ 50% Jade (single factor) + 25% Olive (double factor) + 25% normal.

There is no problem distinguishing the double and single dark factor bird because of their different colours. This tends to indicate that as with the budgerigar there may be three possible shades. In the normal lovebird there is no dark character, while the Olive form has two such characters and the Jade possesses one. It is possible that similar developments will lead to these dark characters emerging in other species, and also in Blue-masked Lovebirds so that mauves and cobalts may eventually be bred.

Establishing a Strain of Mutation Lovebirds

The most efficient method of building up a strain of mutation lovebirds is to purchase a pair of the chosen colour. However, this is expensive and it is likely that some degree of inbreeding will probably have occurred in the foundation stock. There is a risk of a decline in both fertility and type if continued inbreeding takes place, so it could be worth obtaining coloured stock from at least two sources when starting with these birds. The largest and deepest coloured specimens on offer should always be preferred, providing they are healthy.

Recessive Mutations

The pairing of one of the ordinary recessive mutations such as the blue with a normal lovebird will only produce split normals in the first instance. These mutations are more rapidly bred by breeding a blue with a split blue lovebird. In this case, equal proportions of blue and further split birds can be expected. The disadvantage of some pairings is that the split lovebirds cannot be distinguished from the normals, because they are identical in colour, but all normals resulting from the above combination must carry the blue factor.

The cheapest way to begin breeding lovebirds of a sex-linked recessive mutation is, for example, to purchase a lutino cock and pair it with a normal hen of the same species. The chicks from this pairing can be sexed before they leave the nest, because all the females will be lutino, while the males will appear normal, but they must be split for lutino. Having used a normal hen initially, it should be safe to mate the original cock back to his best daughter, so that only lutino chicks will be bred from this combination. At the same time, if the normal hen is paired to one of the split cocks, then approximately one out of every four chicks

*The Angolan form of the Peach-faced Lovebird (*Agapornis roseicol catumbella*).*

will turn out to be a lutino hen. The youngsters from these second generation pairings should not be bred together, and if some are sold or exchanged new blood can be introduced to the strain. Careful inbreeding as described can be beneficial, particularly with regard to improving the depth of colour, but if any signs of weakness appear in the strain, ranging from a relatively high degree of infertility to sickly chicks, unrelated birds must be purchased immediately. Outcrossings using normal lovebirds can be valuable for increasing the size of mutation stock.

Dominant Pied Lovebirds

Any dominant pied paired to a normal will yield a proportion of pied offspring, so to breed these pieds, there need only be one pied parent. Normal coloured birds in a nest with pieds resulting from this pairing could not be split for pied, because this form is dominant, and so therefore must have a normal genotype.

The markings of young pied lovebirds cannot be predicted from the parents, but generally birds with light markings paired together will yield offspring which are similarly marked. In America, pieds with large areas of either white or yellow feathering are most in demand. Lovebirds which appear pure yellow may be bred from pieds but such birds do not subsequently produce pure offspring. It is possible that a standard ideal will be established for pied lovebirds being shown in this country, based perhaps on the requirements for pied budgerigars. Overall, lovebirds with a clear, even depth of colouring are to be preferred to mutations whose coloration appears patchy. Such points should be considered when selecting any of the mutation lovebirds.

Olive and Jade Peach-faced Lovebirds

Jades can be bred either by mating an Olive or a Jade with a normal. All Jades will result from the first pairing, but an equal proportion of Jades and normals should arise from the latter mating. The breeding of Olive lovebirds requires either a Jade paired with an Olive, a pair of Jades, or two Olives mated together. Only half the offspring from the first pairing should be Olive. One in four chicks resulting from Jade parents will be Olive, whereas all the youngsters from the last pairing are Olives. No split lovebirds of either colour can be bred, so all other chicks will be ordinary normals.

The markings of Pied Lovebirds may vary considerably, this one is predominantly green.

Records

The importance of accurate records cannot be overstressed when coloured lovebirds are being bred. Knowledge of their pedigree is vital particularly if more than one pair are kept at any time. Ringing, using split metal rings is useful for separating split lovebirds from normals and possible splits after they leave the nest. Split lovebirds can be rung with anodised aluminium rings while plain aluminium could be used for possible splits. Normals need not be rung. A similar scheme can be devised to recognise coloured birds from different nests if they are not close-rung, or alternatively a system based purely on ring numbers is practical. The advantage of using the first system is that the birds can be identified by sight. A simple breeding register containing such details as the age and ring numbers of the lovebirds will prove invaluable in selecting suitable pairs, and should prevent excessive inbreeding from taking place.

If space and finance permit, it is useful to keep the young lovebirds until they moult out into adult plumage. The final colouring of individual specimens can then be assessed more accurately than when they were in nest feather. There is a much better chance of recognising the most promising birds at this stage rather than disposing of them too early and so missing a 'stormer'.

Hybrid Lovebirds

The breeding of hybrid lovebirds is not universally popular, and such birds find little favour with most serious breeders. Many attractive crosses have been produced however, but the offspring are not always fertile. Young hybrids bred originally from Nyasa and Black-cheeked Lovebirds are a proven exception, and have reproduced successfully themselves. The White eye-ringed group as a whole and the Peach-faced hybridise quite readily, as do mutations of these species. Breeding stock, especially of the new mutations, ought to be kept free of such hybrids because undesirable characteristics might be introduced accidentally in this way and could prove hard to eliminate later.

Chapter 8

Exhibiting

Lovebirds can be seen at most bird shows, and for many breeders such a show provided their first introduction to the group. Lovebirds are not shown in an individual section like budgerigars, but with the increasing number of lovebird mutations now being bred, it may soon be necessary to introduce separate classes within the parrot-like section for these popular birds. There is usually only one class for all lovebirds at many shows today. While ideal standards have been produced for budgerigar and canary breeders for example, no such guidelines are established for the breeders of lovebirds. This is partly because lovebirds have not been bred in such numbers, and as a result there is no specialist society in Britain catering for this section of the Fancy. The condition and steadiness of the lovebird are therefore of paramount importance to the judge, and reflect the ability of an exhibitor to manage his stock successfully.

Lovebirds are not regarded as being good show birds since they often shy away and try to bury themselves in the floor when people, including the judge approach their cage. They may not be as confiding as some other members of the parrot family, but disappointing results on the show bench can often be traced back to inadequate training. It is hopeless to expect a lovebird to win its class when the bird is transferred from an aviary to a show cage and then transported to the unusual surroundings of the show hall, without some form of training.

Stock Training
Steadiness can only be achieved over a period of time and necessitates regular training. Adult lovebirds which have never been shown are very unlikely to steady down sufficiently to make good exhibition birds, even if their plumage is immaculate.

Imported lovebirds will be more suitable for showing if they are kept inside for their first winter, but they are usually handicapped at first by the poor condition of their feathers. They cannot be exhibited until any flight feathers which are clipped have been moulted, and replaced by a new set. It is therefore easier, and for many people more satisfying, to show lovebirds that they have bred themselves.

Training should begin as soon as the youngsters are removed from their parents. The young lovebirds can be housed in a flight cage and if this is put in a position close to where people are walking around, then the birds will become used to people, and should not fly around so wildly when their cage is approached. Care must be taken though to see that the cage, as always, is positioned out of a draught. The steadiest lovebirds can then be selected from the group for the next stage of training. Although the birds may later be shown in pairs, they will be more responsive during these early stages of training if they are housed individually. The next step is to place their flight cage in contact with a show cage, with the doors open so that the lovebirds can move freely from cage to cage. They will be tempted to enter the show cage if a millet spray is hung just inside the door, along with the rest of their food and water. It is however necessary to ensure that they have eaten in these new surroundings.

When the lovebird is used to entering the show cage, the door can be shut leaving the bird inside. At this juncture, it is a good idea to introduce a judging stick to the birds. The judge will move the stick in front of the bars of the cage so that the lovebird turns round and thus the whole of its body can be seen. A piece of dowel or a pencil painted with a glossy white paint will suffice as a judging stick during the training procedure. The lovebirds will probably be disturbed by the stick at first, but when it is used regularly, the bird becomes less scared and eventually will only turn round or move to the next perch as is desired. Talking to the lovebirds while they are caged will help to accustom them to the noise in the show hall.

The length of time required to train the lovebirds will depend on their age and also on their response, because some birds make more natural show specimens than others. A few lovebirds, in spite of all efforts, remain crouched on the floor of the show cage and so cannot hope to win any event regardless of their

*Fischer's Lovebird (*Agapornis fischeri*).*

condition. It may be possible to cure them of this habit by turning the cage upside down, so that the roof now forms the floor of the cage. The roof of a show cage is not flat, but slopes from back to front. It is therefore impossible for a lovebird to bury itself in the far corner of the floor, because it will be unable to get a grip, and slide towards the front of the cage. The bird will then prefer to perch as normal, and should lose its fear, remaining perched when the cage is turned the right way up again.

Show Cages

There are no specific requirements for show cages used for the exhibition of lovebirds. A budgerigar-type show cage is however commonly used, but if a pair of lovebirds are being exhibited a budgerigar team cage is preferred because this gives the birds more space. Even when not exhibiting, it is always useful to visit a local show. This gives a chance to see the standard of the birds, and compare the stock with one's own.

Presentation of the exhibit rightly plays an important part in winning (or losing) at any show. There is no point in showing a perfect specimen in a dirty cage with the paint peeling off the sides, because the bird will not win the class. This part of management is sometimes neglected, but after every show the cage should be thoroughly cleaned, and then it will be ready for the next occupant after being stored in a plastic bag to prevent it becoming dusty and dirty. The cage if treated properly will not need to be painted after each show, but there are times such as at the start of the show season when a new coat of paint is necessary. The outside of the cage is always painted with a black gloss paint, while a safe white emulsion is used on the interior and the bars.

The two perches within the cage are not painted. They should be positioned across the cage from back to front. One perch running the length of the cage is inadequate because it does not often give the judge an opportunity to see the lovebird from all sides, as happens when the bird moves to another perch. The cage itself is not decorated with any greenery, but the floor is usually covered with bird sand. This material is quite absorbent, and if the lovebird gets on to the floor, the sand will help to prevent the feathers from becoming soiled. Each show cage should be equipped with two drinkers, one of which is used for food. No water is normally given until after judging at local shows, because there is a risk that the lovebird will get its plumage wet and matted. Its appearance will therefore be spoilt before the judge has an opportunity to assess the bird's potential. When the show is further afield, birds arriving the night before judging are obviously given water.

Single versus Pairs
An exhibitor of lovebirds can choose to enter his birds either singly or in pairs. A good pair will always win over a single lovebird, but it is futile to exhibit a pair of which only one member is in a suitable condition. Lovebirds such as Fischer's or Masked which are almost impossible to distinguish by sight, need not be shown in true pairs, although this would reduce the risk of squabbling. Birds of either or unknown sex entered individually stand an equal chance, but with regard to the sexually dimorphic species such as the Madagascar, it is very likely that a single cock would be preferred to a hen in similar condition. This is not a case of sex discrimination, but occurs simply because the cock's plumage is more ornate than that of the hen. With these rarer species today however, it may be that there is only one member of a pair in the exhibitor's possession, in which case it will have to be shown singly.

Under some circumstances therefore, it is more prudent to exhibit a lovebird on its own rather than as a member of a pair. A case in point would be a bird which is known to be particularly aggressive, so confining it with another could lead to injuries being sustained by the other member of the pair, especially if the show is longer than a day. A hen Abyssinian Lovebird, having constructed a nest, cannot be shown with a cock until her breast feathers have regrown fully. Indeed with all species, when one member of a pair begins to moult, the chances of the other lovebird will be spoilt if the birds are shown as a pair.

Show Preparation
Once the young lovebirds are relatively steady, they should be released from their flight cages into an aviary where they can develop fully. By this stage they will have been kept in show cages for increasing periods of time up to a day. At the end of this training, it may be possible to enter the young lovebirds in a class

for current year bred parrot-like birds while they are still in nest feather. This gives a chance to see how their training has progressed, because they can be compared with the other entries.

The lovebirds should be assessed again and the final team selected about two weeks or so before a show. The birds chosen are then caught up and placed initially in flight cages. The training procedure is similar to that carried out when the lovebirds were first separated from their parents, except that they should be housed singly or in pairs as decided. In the closer confinement of the cages, it is easier to study the condition of the birds. Their beaks must be clean and should not have eny pieces flaking off when in good condition. Birds with overgrown or deformed beaks are unsuitable for show purposes. A problem with lovebirds is that they are very keen on nipping each other's toes, and adjoining aviaries must be double wired for this reason. A relatively minor injury of this type sees a few spots of blood appear, but in some cases, the birds can easily lose nails or even part of their toes. Such lovebirds once recovered will usually be able to breed, but cannot be shown. Every lovebird must therefore have a full complement of claws, of a normal length, on each foot if it is to win its class. Furthermore, the claws should be of the same colour, because in a few individuals, some nails may be much darker than others. The legs will not normally appear scaly, but if they do, a small amount of olive oil carefully applied with the aid of cotton wool should help to remedy the situation. As a lovebird gets older, its legs will get more heavily scaled.

Spraying and Washing
The feathering of a lovebird will need to look healthy and have a good gloss if it is to catch the judge's eye. Rainwater is accepted as the best natural conditioner for the feathers, and lovebirds living outside have a more attractive 'bloom' than those kept inside permanently. This condition is achieved naturally at least in part by the release of an oily secretion from the preen gland at the base of the back under the feathers, and this substance acts as a waterproofing agent for the plumage. A light spray of water each morning is therefore beneficial just before a show. Various conditioners to improve the plumage are available, and can be added as directed to the water used for spraying. The lovebirds

*n Madagascar Lovebird (*Agapornis cana*).*

should not be sprayed at night, because if they go to roost wet, they may subsequently develop a chill. A light spray also helps to soften the sheaths in which the feathers are wrapped up, and if, just before a show such a spike is visible, it may be removed carefully with the assistance of a wet tissue. This protective covering must not be pulled off, because otherwise the new feather will also be removed and there is an increased risk of bleeding which would ruin the bird's chances.

In a few cases, a lovebird will have a dirty area of plumage particularly if the birds are kept on an earth floor. Although the feathers will have to be washed before the bird is shown, this is not recommended because it will upset the lovebird. If it is practical, the bird should be held in the usual manner and then cotton wool moistened with lukewarm water can be gently rubbed over the dirty area with some soap. Care must be taken especially if the head is being cleaned to ensure that the soap does not enter the eyes. The soap is rinsed out carefully with as little water as possible so that the surrounding feathers do not become saturated. The wet plumage can be wiped over with a dry tissue, and the bird should be left in a relatively warm environment to dry out. Most hospital cages if clean are suitable for drying birds after they have been washed.

Transport to and from Shows

Over recent years, many exhibitors have preferred to travel with their birds to a show if at all possible. Not only does this enable people to meet other fanciers from further afield, making and renewing friendships, but it also reduces the stress on the birds and so increases their chances of winning. For the large shows, many clubs now organise transport for the exhibits of their members and this is a useful service for those who cannot afford the time or money to travel with their entries. If for any reason the lovebirds are being fed on any special food, then this should be tied to the handle of the show cage in a tough paper bag, along with an explanation for the stewards. A plastic bag is unsuitable because dry food may become damp due to condensation on the inside. The floor of the cage should also be covered with seed.

Failing these alternatives, the birds may have to be sent by rail, although there has been a trend for organisers of some shows to refuse to accept rail entries. This is not only because of the increased amount of work involved, but some entries often arrive late after the judging has taken place, and then on rare occasions, unpleasantness has occurred after the event. Enquiries should therefore be made at a local railway station with regard to train times and any packing requirements so that the lovebirds will arrive safely in plenty of time for the show. The cage must be sent with the exhibitor's name, address and telephone number if possible, clearly written on a removable label, along with the destination of the birds. Adequate food must be supplied for the journey, and damp green food or fruit has to suffice as a source of water, although the 'Oasis' bottle drinkers could be a possible alternative. A covering note for the organisers, asking them if they would kindly remove any green food on arrival should also be attached to the cage.

Afterwards
On arrival back from a show, the lovebirds are best released into a flight cage, and supplied with their usual seed, water and green food. A check should be kept on them to ensure that they are eating normally, and after a day or so, the birds can be released back to their usual quarters. If the weather is inclement, they will need to be kept inside until it improves. The chances are that the lovebirds will moult slightly because of the temperature and light differences encountered between the aviary and show hall.

Most shows occur after the breeding season, but showing a good bird too often will undoubtedly affect its breeding performance the next year. A practical system is to show the lovebirds primarily when they are a year old, and then concentrate on breeding from these birds during the following year. The number of shows for each lovebird is largely a matter of experience, and depends partly on their condition. The schedule of showing will also be governed to a great degree by the relative importance of the events. Some exhibitors try their exhibition birds at several local shows, and may then hold one or two back if they are intending to exhibit these at the annual three day National Exhibition held at Alexandra Palace, London each December.

Chapter 9

Ailments and Accidents

Lovebirds are usually healthy birds once acclimatised, and they may live for fifteen years or more. Prevention of disease is invariably much easier than cure, and so every effort should be made to ensure that the birds are housed and fed as well as possible. However, even when kept under ideal conditions, odd cases of injury and illness do arise, and then swift action is necessary to effect a cure. It is often advisable to seek specialist advice from a veterinary surgeon, who will if necessary send blood and faecal samples for laboratory analysis. The accurate diagnosis of many bird ailments without testing is not easy, and the details given below are by no means comprehensive, but they should assist in recognising when a bird is off-colour and in need of attention.

Accidental Injuries
The treatment required depends largely on the severity of the injury. Minor bleeding can be stopped by using a styptic; the application of a cold solution of potash alum on cotton wool or a tissue to the affected area is generally effective. The wound should be cleaned, and a non-toxic ointment such as 'Savlon' may be applied to prevent an infection developing. It is not advisable to cover the injury except in severe cases because a plaster or bandage will irritate the lovebird. The covering will be chewed off and this may worsen the underlying injury.

Damage to the beak can result from fighting, and if a mandible is split, the bird will probably not be able to eat. When the bleeding has ceased an application of non-toxic quick drying dental cement to the outside of the split beak will give support to the tear and should enable the bird to continue eating. If a piece of beak is actually lost, it is advisable to offer a soft food, such as porridge oats mixed with milk and water. Powdered cuttlefish and a vitamin and mineral supplement must also be given, in addition to the normal food.

Lovebirds are relatively small birds, and so every effort should be made to reduce the stress after an accident, since this can kill even though the injury itself may not be too serious. Hence handling must be kept to a minimum. If the injury is severe, it is advisable to keep the bird warm, although this does mean that the patient will need to be satisfactorily reacclimatised before being released back into an outside flight.

Wounds which need stitching require professional attention from a veterinary surgeon, as do suspected bone fractures. If a leg is broken, there is likely to be a noticeable swelling in the region of the break, and the bird will be unwilling to use the limb. A broken wing hangs at an unusual angle and obviously flight over any distance is impossible so that the bird either falls to the floor or clings to the wire when approached. Fractures may require splinting under anaesthesia, and the success of the treatment is largely governed by the region and severity of the break. In some cases when a splint is removed, the leg will have shortened but the bird is not handicapped to any significant degree.

Breeding Ailments
Even the most experienced breeders have cases of egg-binding and feather plucking from time to time. The possible causes of these problems have been discussed earlier, and so this section is concerned with their treatment.

An egg-bound hen cannot expel the egg from her body. The symptoms associated with egg-binding are not specific, but the bird is invariably fluffed-up and distressed. Hens especially at risk are those which have not laid before, or conversely old birds which are not in top breeding condition. Time is a vital factor if treatment is to be effective. The egg can usually be felt by palpitating the vent region very gently. In some cases, transferring the hen to a temperature of about 85°F (29°C) will result in the egg being laid naturally within a few hours.

If the condition of the bird worsens however, it will be necessary to remove the egg by hand. This is a difficult procedure which cannot be hurried and it is advisable to seek preferably the assistance of a veterinary surgeon, or else an experienced breeder. The treatment involves the application of olive oil to the vent, as is suggested later for constipation, although in this case the oil acts as a lubricant to assist the passage of the egg. Gentle pressure is exerted on the egg in the direction of the vent, but it is vital not to break it, because the bird will then die from peritonitis. Soft shelled or abnormally shaped eggs which may have caused the egg-binding initially make the procedure even more difficult.

When the egg is removed safely, the bird should be left to recover in warm and quiet surroundings, with food and water provided within easy reach. The treatment is of necessity drastic, and fatalities may occur simply because of the stress involved. In some cases, paralysis of the legs is noticeable, but hopefully this will only be transitory and the bird's condition should be dramatically improved within a week. Once recovered, a young hen must not be bred from again for at least a year.

With regard to feather plucking, there is sadly nothing that can be done to speed the growth of new feathers. An old fancier's remedy to dissuade a cock or hen from plucking their youngsters is to apply finely powdered bitter aloes to the chick's body feathers only. In some cases, this treatment proves effective, presumably because the lovebird dislikes the taste of aloes although birds do not have a highly developed sense of taste. Various aerosol sprays are also available for the prevention of feather plucking but they do not always work successfully. If bruising is noticed on the chick's skin, it can be relieved by an application of a non-toxic lotion such as 'Astral' hand cream. Some fanciers swear that this encourages more rapid feather growth, but the case is still open to dispute!

Digestive Ailments

Lovebirds do not usually suffer from digestive disturbances if they are fed correctly, and kept under clean conditions. Stale green food, dirty water and lack of a suitable sized grit are common causes of digestive upsets which can be easily eliminated by good management.

Constipation is especially likely to arise from a shortage of grit which, as already mentioned, is necessary for correct digestion of food. When suffering from constipation, a bird is unable to pass any droppings and will be seen straining from the perch. An

Hen Abyssinian or Black-winged Lovebird (Agapornis tarar

effective and simple remedy is to massage olive oil around the vent. The oil acts as a lubricant, enabling the dry faeces to be voided more easily. It is conveniently applied on a paper tissue, but take care not to apply it over too wide an area, because the oil will stain and mat the feathers, giving them an unsightly appearance. Fresh green food supplied in moderation will assist this treatment, and given regularly, it should help to prevent the complaint reoccurring. Various cures for constipation are sold by most pet stores, but always ensure that the instructions on the pack are followed implicitly during use.

Diarrhoea may occur after an attack of constipation, or vice-versa often because the natural rhythm of the gut has been disturbed. Alternatively, a common mistake is to overfeed green food, and this invariably results in diarrhoea. However many other complaints can cause diarrhoea, some of which are both serious and infectious, and so a veterinary surgeon should be contacted without delay. This is especially important if blood appears in the droppings, which in the case of a bird suffering from diarrhoea become loose and may change in colour. Staining around the vent is indicative of a digestive disorder. Birds with diarrhoea will want to drink more water, since they must compensate for the increased amount of fluid which is being lost in their droppings.

Many digestive tract infections can now be treated with antibiotics, although tests may be necessary to discover the most effective drug for a particular complaint. More details about the supply and use of antibiotics are given later in this chapter.

Eye Ailments

Although birds suffering from eye ailments are unmistakable, the cause of the trouble is not so easily identified. The eye will appear inflamed and there may be a watery discharge on to the feathers which thus appear matted. The bird will often blink more than usual and rubs its head frequently on surrounding perches. Some eye complaints are contagious and so an affected bird must be isolated immediately.

A veterinary surgeon should be contacted especially if both eyes are affected and there is also a nasal discharge. It is always advisable to wash one's hands thoroughly after handling any sick bird, but this is particularly important when eye complaints are involved, because some may be directly transmitted to Man. Apart from infections, irritants and draughts are possible underlying reasons for eye inflammation.

The treatment obviously depends on the cause of the complaint. Boracic acid lotion can be applied to relieve an irritation and ophthalmic antibiotic ointments have proved very successful in combating most infections. Any such ointment must be specifically for eye treatment, and so will be labelled ophthalmic. The ointment is gently smeared on the affected eye or its eyelids, but if the bird is then released immediately, the chances are that most of the preparation will be rubbed off on a convenient perch! Holding the patient for a couple of minutes after application of the ointment will enable some to dissolve in the eye fluid and reach the source of infection. After the bird has had a course of treatment the ointment should be disposed of, because it does not keep indefinitely.

Lumps

Lumps visible outside the body require veterinary treatment. Such growths, more correctly known as tumours, can be divided into two groups. Those which grow slowly in one place are regarded as benign whilst others which spread throughout the body are known as malignant or cancerous tumours. Depending on the site and type of the growth, it may be possible to have the tumour removed surgically, and a veterinary surgeon is best qualified to make this decision for the owner.

The causes of such growths are not clear, but experience with budgerigars and canaries suggests there could be a genetic link, because some strains have a higher occurrence of tumours than others. Tumours can occur almost anywhere on the body, but they may not be visible until the feathers are pushed aside.

Internal tumours will only be confirmed by post-mortem examination if they do not grow out from an organ and subsequently distort the skin. A relatively common site for such growths is the ovary, and here they may result in a partial sex change. Indeed there is even a case on record of a hen which became a cockerel and then mated successfully with another hen! This is however exceptional and in most birds, a hen with an ovarian tumour will not lay or accept advances from a cock. Yet a growth is by no means the only cause of such behaviour although in the sexually dimorphic species, if a hen begins to assume male plumage, such a tumour is very likely.

A lovebird sometimes suddenly loses weight, although externally it appears quite normal. Under such circumstances, a serious internal malfunction, perhaps caused by a tumour, is indicated and treatment is of no avail. When a bird dies under these circumstances, a post-mortem examination will only be of value if the body reaches the laboratory in good condition as quickly as possible after death. Regulations governing the packaging and dispatch of dead birds vary from country to country, but details can be obtained from major post offices. Concise information about the bird, such as its age, origins and recent history, is often of value to a laboratory.

Overgrown Beaks and Claws
Lovebirds rarely need to have their claws or beaks cut, especially if they have access to wooden perches of various diameters, and it is not a task to be undertaken lightly. Apart from the upset caused by catching the bird, cutting of the claws and beak often encourages them to regrow at a faster rate. Comparison with

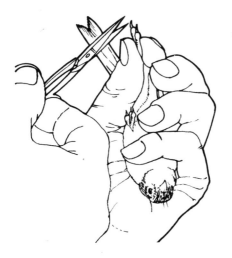

The correct way to trim a bird's claws.

other lovebirds is useful before reaching a decision about cutting, and the advice of an experienced fancier is invaluable in this respect. In certain circumstances there is no alternative because the bird will be unable to eat if its beak curls any further, while overgrown claws may result in a bird getting caught up and injuring itself.

Cutting the claws is a relatively simple task using either a sharp pair of scissors or preferably special bone clippers. When viewed in good light, a thin red line can be seen running part of the way down the claw. This is a blood vessel and so the cut must be made a short distance after the disappearance of the vein, otherwise bleeding will occur. When clipping a bird's claw for the first time, it is helpful if someone else holds the bird, because this leaves both hands free to concentrate on cutting the claw correctly.

The beak is cut in a similar manner, after the blood supply has been located. The top mandible should never be cut back above the level of the lower beak, but if in any doubt ask a veterinary surgeon for assistance.

Parasites
Parasites are usually divided into two categories. Ectoparasites including various mites and lice are found on the feathers and skin, while endoparasites such as respiratory mites and worms of the intestinal tract live within the body of the bird.

Most birds have a constant population of minute ectoparasites even when they are in fact healthy. Yet the number of parasites increases when a bird is weakened or diseased and new stock should always be sprayed. Special safe aerosol sprays which kill mites and lice on birds are sold in most pet shops, and regular spraying helps to ensure that the numbers of ectoparasites are controlled. Various preparations are also available for keeping the bird's quarters free of these pests, and certainly cleanliness reduces the risk of a parasite explosion. Needless to say, all parasites are easily transmitted to healthy stock.

Red mite, known scientifically as *Dermanyssus gallinae* is a relatively common parasite, especially on feral sparrows which may be attracted by loose seed to an aviary and so transmit mite to the lovebirds within. The mites do not always live on the birds permanently, but often emerge at night from surrounding corners and crevices to feed on their blood. Hence a bird infested with mite will lose weight, its general condition will deteriorate and it may start to pluck its feathers.

Lovebirds are particularly at risk if they are allowed to roost and breed in the same nestbox year after year. It is advisable to change the box after the breeding season, and treat it and the birds as instructed with a suitable preparation. Obviously, merely spraying the birds if an outbreak of red mite occurs is not likely to be satisfactory. Mites are able to exist for months without coming into contact with a bird and so treatment of infected accommodation must be very thorough, and repeated at intervals before it can be considered safe to return the birds. Although red mites are smaller than a pin head, they can be seen easily if an infected cage is covered with a white cloth. They will emerge in the dark, and become visible against the white background when the cloth is examined.

Endoparasitic infections are difficult to treat successfully because the drugs available are liable to prove toxic, especially when the birds have already been weakened by the presence of the parasites. Lovebirds kept in enclosures with grass or earth floors are more likely to succumb to a variety of endoparasites such as roundworms, than are birds living above a concrete or gravel base. Analysis of the droppings should reveal if a bird is suffering from internal parasites. Although it is sometimes possible to worm the birds regularly as a preventative measure, this is also a somewhat hazardous procedure, and so veterinary advice should be sought beforehand.

Psittacosis

When psittacosis was first identified in 1879, it was thought that only parrots carried the disease, yet subsequent research has shown that any bird can be infected, and so the description of ornithosis is perhaps more applicable. The disease can be transmitted to Man, producing pneumonia-like symptoms, and until the advent of antibiotics, it did not respond to treatment.

Newly imported birds are most likely to be infected, but the disease should develop within their period of quarantine before they are sold. Infected birds appear lifeless and fluffed up, with a discharge from the eyes and nostrils as well as severe diarrhoea. Once again, these symptoms are not diagnostic, but a veterinary surgeon must be called in if this disease is suspected. Treatment should not be attempted, and the stock will have to be destroyed. Thankfully psittacosis occurs very rarely, and if the stock is well-established, the disease is unlikely to develop suddenly.

Respiratory Problems

The breathing movements of a lovebird provide a useful clue to its overall state of health. In a fit bird, the respiratory rate is about 130 beats per minute which is really too high to count under normal circumstances. Yet it is possible to assess their rate of breathing from the slight tail movements which accompany the intake and expiration of air. If these tail movements appear faster than normal, the lovebird has either been subjected to stress, or else it may be unwell. This change can usually be observed when a bird is caught and transferred to a cage, yet in this case the breathing soon returns to normal. Alternatively, the rate can be slowed down or become irregular and a bird which is having difficulty in breathing will often keep its beak open, and respiratory movements may be accompanied by wheezing. A loss of appetite and fluffing of the feathers indicate that the condition is serious, and any bird so afflicted should be isolated, because the complaint may be contagious. There are many possible reasons for such distress and again the experience of a veterinary surgeon should prove invaluable in isolating the cause rapidly. Several possible causes are given below of which infection by a wide range of bacteria, viruses, fungi and parasites is probably the most significant.

Aspergillosis, for example, is caused by a fungus, the spores of which are inhaled by the bird and subsequently develop in the respiratory system. The air passageways, lungs and air sacs become blocked by the growth of the fungus, and so the bird has difficulty breathing. It is a highly contagious condition.

Confirmation of the diagnosis can only be made at post-mortem and so professional advice should be sought without delay. No successful treatment is yet available, but at the time of writing, a vaccine being developed at the Willamette Animal and Medical Laboratory, Portland, Oregon in the United States has proved successful in clinical trials over the last two and a half years, and so may soon be available commercially.

The risk of *Aspergillus* infection is dramatically increased if the birds are kept under damp conditions and fed on dirty, dusty seed, which again emphasises the importance of good management in the prevention of disease. Damp hay is a likely source of the spores and so this should not be supplied as nesting material, especially because of the high degree of humidity which must be maintained to ensure that the chicks hatch satisfactorily. Aspergillosis appears to develop particularly when birds are exposed to stress, and so isolation of newly acquired stock is always advisable.

Poor ventilation of the bird's surroundings may result in respiratory problems because fumes are likely to build up in a confined space. This point should be remembered before using an oil or paraffin heater in a birdroom, since if the night is cold, the ventilation will have already been reduced to a minimum to prevent unnecessary heat loss. Internal injuries, or growths which exert pressure on part of the respiratory system can also interfere with breathing, but treatment of these causes is highly unlikely to be successful.

Guidelines for Treatment
It is obvious from the above that while diagnosis of bird diseases is best undertaken by a veterinary surgeon, the success of treatment often depends on the owner.

Many birds respond to heat when they are ill. A hospital cage is useful for such emergencies since a temperature in the region of 85°–90°F (29°–32°C) can be easily maintained, because the cage heating is thermostatically controlled. In addition, the thermostat setting can be altered, enabling the bird to be gradually reacclimatised once it has recovered.

Modern drugs, especially antibiotics have proved valuable in all fields of medicine, including the treatment of bird diseases. The actual regulations governing the supply of antibiotics vary from one country to another. In Great Britain, antibiotics cannot be bought, but must be obtained on prescription from a veterinary surgeon, whereas in America many treatments containing antibiotics are sold in pet stores.

Antibiotics for internal use are dispensed either in the form of a powder which is added to the drinking water, or as seed impregnated with the drug. A sick bird will often drink although it may have lost its appetite, and so an additive for the water is perhaps the most effective remedy. It is however vital to give the correct dosage, which should be stated on the container, because otherwise more harm than good will result. Underdosing will prove ineffective, while overdosing can kill both beneficial and harmful organisms, and so lowers the bird's resistance to another infection. Water treated with drugs should never be provided in metal drinkers, because a chemical reaction may occur with the metal altering the action of the drug. Glass or china containers are quite safe for use.

Many experienced fanciers feel that they can attend to the majority of the problems which afflict their stock without reference to a veterinary surgeon. However, it is much better for the beginner to seek professional advice when a bird is ill, because although this will cost money, it will be a relatively small outlay compared to the loss of a bird through incorrect or inadequate treatment. There is little point in waiting for a day or so before seeking advice if a bird is ill, because by this time it is likely that any treatment will prove ineffective, and then not only does the bird die, but the consultancy fee is also wasted. Some veterinary surgeons have more experience of dealing with birds than others and so when making enquiries in the neighbourhood, it is worth bearing this point in mind.

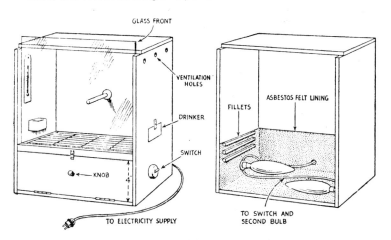

GLASS FRONT

VENTILATION HOLES

DRINKER

SWITCH

KNOB

TO ELECTRICITY SUPPLY

FILLETS

ASBESTOS FELT LINING

TO SWITCH AND SECOND BULB

A glass-fronted hospital cage with exposed heating arrangements.

Chapter 10

The Species

Introduction

Lovebirds can be broadly divided into two categories, with the Peach-faced being regarded as an intermediate form between the sexually dimorphic and White eye-ringed groups. The Black-collared Lovebird is probably another intermediate type, although little is known about this species. The Madagascar, Red-faced and Abyssinian Lovebirds which have certain characteristics in common, are thought to be the closest related species to the original ancestors of the group which developed north of the equator in the sub-tropical zone of Africa. They are distinguished as the sexually dimorphic group because their plumage varies according to the sex of the bird. All cocks of these species have black on the tail and underwing coverts, apart from other more specific coloration differences.

Hen lovebirds of this type only carry nesting material tucked in amongst their feathers, whereas the White eye-ringed group use their beaks for this purpose. Cross-breeding between the two forms has revealed that such behaviour is inherited in lovebirds. A Peach-faced Lovebird was crossed with a Fischer's and the resulting offspring were subsequently unsure as to how to carry nesting material. They tried to tuck it in between the feathers of the rump and lower back, like true Peach-faced Lovebirds, but it kept falling out. However, by the time that they were three years old, the birds had learnt to carry it in their beaks or in amongst their feathers. This behaviour is not seen in true members of the White eye-ringed group.

The latter group build a more elaborate nest which is domed in shape, whereas the sexually dimorphic lovebirds use smaller pieces of material to construct a basic pad for their eggs. Their chicks hatch covered in white down and develop relatively slowly whereas young White eye-ringed (and Peach-faced) Lovebirds emerge from the egg with a coat of red down and grow at a somewhat faster rate.

The Classification of Lovebirds
Lovebirds were originally included in a much larger genus known as *Psittacus* until 1836, when Selby in his work on *Parrots* (pages 117–118) placed them in a separate genus *Agapornis*. Species such as the Masked Lovebird which were first discovered after this date were immediately given the generic name *Agapornis*. People who had previously categorised lovebirds as members of the *Psittacus* genus have their names bracketed after the scientific name of the bird to indicate the change in the nomenclature.

The scientific description of every lovebird begins with the generic name *Agapornis*, written with a capital letter. This is followed by the specific name which indicates the actual species of lovebird, and together these two terms constitute the binomial classification. When there are two or more races which are similar but not identical, it is necessary to add a third term to distinguish between the subspecies, and this is why the trinomial classification is popular with scientists today. In the case of the Madagascar Lovebird for example, its full scientific description is *Agapornis cana cana*, and since *cana* is repeated, this form can be recognised as the nominate or typical race. Another subspecies, known as *Agapornis cana ablectanea* is recognised on grounds of its slightly different coloration. The classification used in this chapter is based on Peters' *Check-List of Birds of the World*, 1931, except where stated to the contrary.

THE SEXUALLY DIMORPHIC GROUP

RED-FACED LOVEBIRD – *Agapornis pullaria pullaria*
   (Linnaeus, also known as Von Linné).
Reference: *Systema Naturae,* tenth edition, page 102. Date: 1758.
Source of original specimen: Formerly thought to be Asia and Ethiopia but this was incorrect. Neumann subsequently suggested Ghana.

*A pair of Red-faced Lovebirds (*Agapornis pullaria*) with their darker-beaked youngster in the centre.*

Distribution: Western part of equatorial Africa; countries east of Sierra Leone to Lake Albert in Uganda, extending into northern Angola.

Length: 6 inches (15 cm).

Cock: Body mainly light green, more yellow underneath. Orange-red feathering prominent on the head. Rump feathers blue; black flight feathers and underwing coverts. Tail green, mixed with red, yellow and black markings. Red beak; feet and legs greyish. Brown irises.

Hen: Similar coloration but paler, and head feathering more orange than red. Green underwing coverts with yellower edges to the wings.

Young Birds: Similar to the hen, but red areas even paler. They can however still be sexed by the characteristic difference in the colour of the underwing coverts.

Number of eggs and incubation period: Three to six eggs should hatch after about twenty-three days although Emin records only two to three eggs.

OTHER SUBSPECIES

A.p. ugandae Neumann.

Reference: *Nov. Zool.*, page 388. Date: 1908.

Source of original specimen: Entebbe, Uganda.

Distribution: More easterly part of the range. Uganda and the Omo River region extending south to Rwanda.

Difference from nominate race: Deeper coloured blue rump.

Number of eggs end incubation period: As above.

Luke stated that the heads of Red-faced Lovebirds, with their somewhat elongated beaks reminded him of the *Brotogeris* parrakeets from South America, which include the relatively common Canary-winged (*B. versicolorus chiriri*) and Orange-flanked Parrakeets (*B. pyrrhopterus*). This similarity is not perhaps entirely surprising when it is considered that all these birds have been observed nesting in termitaria in the wild.

Red-faced Lovebirds excavate their breeding chambers in termite nests which may be located up to 40 feet (12 metres) above the ground in trees. Only on rare occasions is a terrestrial termite mound used by these birds. Although the termites are normally savage if their home is approached, they appear to readily accept both the excavations and continued presence of the lovebirds. The lovebirds probably choose a site away from the living quarters of the termite's nest, so that both populations can exist without coming into conflict with each other. The termites themselves feed on the cellulose contained in the trees and other vegetation, so that the adult birds and chicks are not likely to be molested in their breeding chamber. The termites may offer the lovebirds an increased degree of protection against predators.

The Red-faced Lovebird is found inland where there are areas of grassland interspersed with woodland. They forage for food eating grass seeds and figs, before returning to roost in trees at night. It has the widest range of any lovebird and in some areas, comes into contact with other species, but hybrids have not been reported. Red-faced lovebirds can cause a lot of damage to crops when they descend in flocks of twenty or more, and so are frequently persecuted by the natives.

Breeding results have only been obtained in captivity on a very few occasions with this species. Although included in portraits dating back over four hundred years, it was not until 1956 that the Red-faced Lovebird bred successfully for the first time in Europe. A. A. Prestwich published a detailed account of this breeding in the *Avicultural Magazine* of January 1957 which earned him an Avicultural Medal. He supplied small wooden barrels, about 14 inches (35 cm) by 12 inches (30 cm) which had been filled with wet peat, to his colony of Red-faced Lovebirds. Once the peat had set hard, the barrels were positioned horizontally against the sides of the flight. The bottom half of the exposed face was partially covered with wood to prevent all the contents falling out on to the aviary floor.

The hen lovebirds were primarily responsible for excavating the burrows which led upwards to expand into a chamber about 4 inches (10 cm) in diameter. Here the eggs were laid, and later it emerged that no nesting material had been used by the birds. One chick was reared to maturity by a pair of Prestwich's birds. Other aviculturists have subsequently constructed artificial termite nests for this species using compressed peat bales. The lovebirds can then dig out their nesting chamber, although several inches should be removed from the exposed face to form a slight hole from which the birds may continue excavating. Some reports suggest that Red-faced Lovebirds use only fresh leaves in their nest, and this may be another reason why breeding is not often successful in captivity. Branches with leaves attached should be placed in water and offered fresh to these birds.

Prestwich recorded that his birds did not roost in their breeding quarters, but hung upside down from the top of the aviary, like Hanging Parrots (*Loriculus*). This behaviour has not been noted by every aviculturist who has kept this species, and as with all lovebirds, the Red-faced must be allowed access to its nesting site for roosting purposes throughout the year. These lovebirds should be discouraged from hanging on the wire in the outside flight if there is likely to be a frost, because they may lose their toes from frost-bite.

Very few Red-faced Lovebirds are available today, partly because they have proved so difficult to breed in captivity. They have gained a reputation for being a somewhat delicate member of the genus when first imported, and so if they become more widely available again, only the most vigorous specimens should be chosen. It would be wiser to bring them inside for their first winter in this country. They are not very active birds and enjoy climbing about their quarters, often in preference to flying. The Red-faced Lovebird is gentler than some of its relations, and in a sufficiently large aviary, several pairs can be kept together, although there is always a risk that one individual will become troublesome. In the past, birds of this species were popular on the show bench, but many are of a nervous disposition when first imported.

MADAGASCAR LOVEBIRD – *Agapornis cana cana* (Gmelin).
Reference: *Systema Naturae* Part 1, page 350. Date: 1788.
Source of original specimen: Malagasy.

Alternative names: Grey-headed or Lavender-headed Lovebird.

Distribution: Found naturally on most of the island of Malagasy (formerly Madagascar) but it has been introduced to neighbouring islands including Mauritius, Comoro Island, Mafia and Zanzibar.

Length: 5 inches (13 cm).

Cock: Head, throat and neck greyish in colour. Remainder of the body green, which is darker on the wings. The beak is light grey, as are the feet. Green tail banded with black. Irises are brown.

Hen: Easily distinguished from the cock because there is no grey on the head. This is replaced by green plumage.

Young Birds: Resemble adults. The grey seen in cocks has a greenish tinge around the necks of youngsters.

Number of eggs and incubation period: Three to eight eggs incubated for twenty-three days.

OTHER SUBSPECIES

A.c. ablectanea. Bangs.

Reference: *Bulletin of the Museum of Comparative Zoology*, page 503. Date: 1918.

Source of original specimen: Morondava Delta.

Distribution: Dry south-western region of Malagasy.

Difference from nominate race: Darker green colouring overall, and the grey coloration of the cock's head is more clearly defined.

Number of eggs and incubation period: As above.

This species is hardly ever seen in collections today because in common with all fauna, its export from its native country is now banned. Unlike the previous species, the Madagascar Lovebird is

109

◄ *Madagascar Lovebird.*

a bird of the forest, and flocks numbering several hundred birds have been reported after the breeding season. The flocks split up at breeding time, and pairs nest individually rather than as part of a colony.

Few other observations have been made about these lovebirds in the wild. The only breeding behaviour noted in the field is of four cock birds which flew individually to a tree hole, bowed and then offered food to the hen at the entrance. They are said to feed largely on rice and are thus unpopular with the natives. It may be worth offering rice to any newly imported stock, and as an addition to the diet at breeding time. Many specimens have been imported in the past, but they are not always easy birds to establish in confinement.

The subspecies from the south-west of the island is the only example of a lovebird which has evolved in a different environment, instead of occurring because of isolation. Madagascar Lovebirds have the smallest beak of the genus, but they can use it most effectively when handled without care. It has been suggested that their beak has developed in conjunction with their diet which does not include thick-shelled tree seeds.

Madagascar Lovebirds have proved to be shy birds in captivity, and do not reproduce as freely as some other species. Coming from a forest setting, they probably require more privacy during the breeding season, but once they go to nest, more than one round of chicks may be reared during the year. A natural log nestbox should tempt a reticent pair to lay before too long. This species also requires leafy branches as nesting material and may choose either dry or fresh leaves to line its nest. When breeding, these birds should not be disturbed because they are likely to abandon their nest.

As with all lovebirds, the hen incubates alone, and later if the cock is seen entering the box during the day, it can be safely assumed that there are chicks within. The hen will only emerge to be fed regularly by the cock when the youngsters are at least a fortnight old. When the chicks hatch, they are covered in a light white down, which becomes dark grey as they grow older. The young lovebirds may leave the nest as early as forty days after hatching, and although young hens are difficult to distinguish from adult birds, the grey heads of immature cocks are suffused with green.

The cock feeds the youngsters when they leave the nest, but he may soon grow tired of his sons. All the young birds should be removed as soon as they are independent, although the cocks may need to be taken away beforehand to escape father's wrath. Outside the breeding season, pairs are fairly amenable together but when in breeding condition, hens are especially aggressive and so it is safer to house these birds in separate pairs. No interbreeding has been recorded with other species, but this may simply be because the Madagascar Lovebird is not freely available.

ABYSSINIAN LOVEBIRD – *Agapornis taranta taranta* (Stanley).

Reference: *Salt's Voyages in Abyssinia*, appendix 4 page 52. Date: 1814.

Source of original specimen: Pass of Taranta in Ethiopia commemorated in their scientific name.

Alternative name: Black-winged Lovebird.

Distribution: Central and Eastern parts of Ethiopia, also southern region of Eritrea.

Length: 6½ inches (16·5 cm).

Cock: Characteristic bright red markings on the forehead and a band around the eyes. The red feathering on the head is not therefore as extensive as in the case of the Red-faced Lovebird. Remainder of the body is green, but the flight feathers and underwing coverts are brownish black. The tail feathers also have a black bar near their tips. Red beak; brown irises and grey legs and feet.

Hen: Lacks the red forehead and black wing markings of the

cock, and so is basically green in colour, darker on the wings.

Young Birds: Can be recognised by their yellow beaks.

Number of eggs and incubation period: Three to six eggs incubated for about twenty-three days.

OTHER SUBSPECIES

A.t. nana Neumann.

Reference: *Journal of Ornithology*, page 550. Date: 1931.

Source of original specimen: North of Targa, Gofa, Ethiopia.

Distribution: South-western Ethiopia.

Difference from nominate race: Smaller beak and shorter wings.

Number of eggs and incubation period: As above, but may be double-brooded.

These lovebirds occur at a relatively high altitude ranging from 6,000–10,000 feet (1800–3000 metres) where the temperature is much lower than at sea level. This probably accounts for the relative hardiness of Abyssinian Lovebirds once they are acclimatised. They are more readily available at present than the other members of the sexually dimorphic group, but cannot be described as common.

In spite of the ease with which these lovebirds can be sexed, it has proved difficult to persuade them to breed in captivity and this may be related to the fact that they are birds of the forest, nesting high up in trees. The hen Abyssinian Lovebird is unique in losing most of her breast feathers before she lays, and these feathers form a soft lining in the nest which is constructed largely from pieces of bark. It is not clear if the hen's feathers are moulted naturally, or whether they are plucked out. The feathers regrow after the breeding season, and only then can the hen be exhibited again with her mate.

When the chicks hatch, they are covered in a light white down which becomes dark grey as they grow older, like the offspring of other members of this group. Young Abyssinian Lovebirds leave the nest when they are seven weeks old. At this time, their beaks are yellow in colour but they change gradually to the red colour of the adult birds. It is not possible to sex these lovebirds reliably however until they have completed their first moult, by the time

113

ock Abyssinian or Black-winged Lovebird.

they are about nine months old. All Abyssinians in immature plumage resemble adult hens, but it has been suggested that young males have some flecks of red feathering on their heads, and their underwing coverts are darker than those of females. If no red feathering is visible when the birds are a year old, they can safely be assumed to be hens.

Some breeders feel that there is a distinct difference between the breeding habits of the nominate race and the subspecies. The true Abyssinian Lovebird may only breed once a year, while the subspecies found especially in mountainous regions, can have two or more rounds of chicks and might not use nesting material. This latter observation however must be regarded as doubtful and suitable material always supplied, although the feathers of the hen bird could prove an adequate substitute to form the pad on which the eggs are laid. The Abyssinian Lovebird is one of the hardier species but cocks are less vigorous than hens and it may take a year or two before the birds attempt to raise a family. They might appear relatively slow, inoffensive and quiet, but these birds can be particularly vicious if housed with other lovebirds. Apples and figs are often especially popular with Abyssinian Lovebirds.

THE INTERMEDIATE GROUP

SWINDERN'S BLACK-COLLARED LOVEBIRD – *Agapornis swinderniana swinderniana*. (Kuhl).
Reference: *Nova Acta Acad. Caes. Leop. Carol.,* page 62 and plate 2. Date: 1820.
Source of original specimen: Liberia.
Alternative name: Liberian Lovebird.

Distribution: Liberia, confined to the tropical rain forests. Early 1977 reported from Ghana.

114

*Swindern's Black-collared Lovebird (*Agapornis swindernian

Length: 5¼ inches (13·5 cm).

Sexes: Similar in appearance. Predominantly green in colour, with a characteristic black half collar at the base of the neck. Chrome yellow feathers below the collar extending round to the edge of the chest. Rump, upper tail colours and lower tail are bright blue. The flight feathers are black. Tail feathers green, intermingled with red. The irises are yellow, the beak is dark horn coloured and the feet and legs are grey.

Young Birds: Recognised by the absence of a complete collar.

Number of eggs and incubation period: Unknown.

OTHER SUBSPECIES

A.s. zenkeri. Reichenow.

Reference: *Orn. Monatsb.*, page 112. Date: 1895.

Source of original specimen: Jaunde in the Cameroon.

Distribution: Cameroon to Central Zaire (formerly the Congo).

Difference from nominate race: The area of yellow around the collar is replaced by orange feathering, and overall the body colour is a darker green.

Number of eggs and incubation period: Unknown.

A.s. emini. Neumann.

Reference: *Bulletin of the British Ornithologists' Club*, page 42. Date: 1908.

Source of original specimen: Ituri Forest.

Distribution: Ituri and Semliki districts of Zaire.

Difference from *A.s. zenkeri*: Reduced area of orange feathering, and the beak is more curved. Flight feathers may be of a different length.

Number of eggs and incubation period: Unknown.

Note: James Chapin (1939) considered that Peters' separation of *emini* from *zenkeri* was not valid. Further study is necessary to solve this controversy. Some authorities feel that there is a difference in the habits of the subspecies. In the Ituri district, where *emini* is said to occur, these birds are found near crops of sesame and rice fields.

Swindern's Black-collared Lovebird was named after a Swedish doctor called van Swinderen. The species became known as *A. swinderniana* apparently because of a spelling mistake, and once this was realised, it was then impossible to alter the established name of the bird. These lovebirds may overlap in certain parts of their range with the Red-faced Lovebird, which occurs on the edges of the dense forest in which they live.

The Black-collared Lovebird appears to be rare in the wild and is virtually unknown in captivity. Few observations about the life of these birds have been recorded, and they are not easy to identify because their colour and small size enables them to merge into the green background of the forest. Black-collared Lovebirds live in small groups, numbering up to a dozen birds. They are seen around their roosting trees during the early morning and evening, calling to each other in a shrill twitter. These lovebirds spend some time on the ground, and insects discovered in their crops may form a relatively important part of their diet.

Nothing is known about their breeding habits, only that the black collar is absent in young birds which have just left the nest, and the area of yellow feathering is reduced in size. Dr. Buttekofer found that the only semblance of the collar was a few black feathers on each side of the neck, while the overall coloration was a duller green than the adult. The beak is lighter in colour in immature birds, complete with a small black spot at its base. There is no record of these lovebirds being imported into Europe, but a few may have reached America. If an aviculturist is lucky enough to obtain Black-collared Lovebirds, every effort should be made to breed them, and any information concerning their behaviour ought to be recorded for subsequent publication by one of the specialist magazines.

Whole fresh figs should be readily accepted by Black-collared Lovebirds when they are first acquired, and probably form the basis of their diet in the wild. Failing access to a fresh supply, dried figs soaked in water and a wide range of fruit plus mealworms may prove suitable alternatives for these birds. They have been said to ignore seeds in captivity, but with perseverance, it might be possible to persuade them to sample millet sprays and other small seeds, while always providing figs and fruit daily.

Father Hutsebout, who observed and kept these birds in their native country, felt that they were specialised seed-eaters rather than strict frugivores. He pointed to the fact that these lovebirds ate the pips of the figs, discarding the fruit itself and so he did not think that they would survive for long in an area where figs were not available throughout the year. In his experience, they only survived up to four days without figs. This is hardly surprising if the lovebirds were not carefully weaned on to an alternative diet, still supplemented with figs. As with other parrot-like birds, it may simply be that Black-collared Lovebirds prefer the pips and when naturally supplied with a constant abundance of figs, they ignore the fruit itself.

PEACH-FACED LOVEBIRD – *Agapornis roseicollis roseicollis.*
(Vieillot)
Reference: *Nouv. Dict. Hist. Nat.*, page 377. Date: 1817.
Source of original specimen: Interior of the Cape of Good Hope.
Alternative name: Rosy-faced lovebird.

Distribution: South-western Africa.

Length: 6 inches (15 cm).
Sexes: Similar in appearance. Pink around the head extending down under the throat to the breast. Blue feathers on the lower back. Remainder of body feathers light green in colour, but darker on the wings. Tail green, interspersed with red, black and blue markings. Flight feathers black. Irides brown, beak horn coloured. Feet and legs grey. Hens perhaps may be recognised because their heads are paler.
Young Birds: Some black may be visible on the upper

118

mandible. Duller coloration overall, lacking the pink
markings of the adult bird.
Number of eggs and incubation period: Three to six eggs
incubated for twenty-three days.

OTHER SUBSPECIES
A.r. catumbella. Hall.
Reference: Skins were shown by Mrs. Hall to members of the
British Ornithologists' Club. Date: 1955.
Source of original specimen: Benguella region of Angola.
Distribution: South Angola.
Difference from nominate race: A deeper coloration all over
the body, which calls into question the theory that hen
birds can be selected because of their paler colouring.
Number of eggs and incubation period: As above.
Note: This subspecies was not recognised by Peters.

Peach-faced Lovebirds inhabit arid country where they live
together in small groups, ranging up to an altitude of 5,000 feet
(1,500 metres) above sea level. Seeds and berries form the basis
of their diet, and they rarely stray any distance from water. In
Africa, Peach-faced Lovebirds will use nests made by weavers,
favourites being those of the Sociable and Mahali weavers,
(*Philetairus socius* and *Plocepasser mahali*), to which the hen
adds more material, forming a cup in the inside of the nest, in
which she lays her eggs. Weaver nests may form suitable nesting
receptacles in captivity, but boxes are usually offered in
preference. The young are covered with thick red down when
they hatch, and they leave the nest when they are just over six
weeks old, developing slower than members of the White eye-
ringed group. The breeding season extends from February to
March, and they are found nesting in colonies at this time.
When these lovebirds were first discovered in 1793, they were
thought to be a form of the Red-faced Lovebird, and it was only in
1817 that they were identified correctly as a separate species.
Peach-faced Lovebirds may be in a transitional stage of evolution.
They resemble the more primitive sexually dimorphic group by
lacking an area of white skin around the eyes, and yet the sexes
cannot be distinguished on sight, so that the pelvic bone test
remains the only reliable guide. Furthermore their habit of

carrying nesting material in their feathers suggests an affinity to this group, although only the feathers of the back and rump are used. This behaviour was first noted in captivity when these lovebirds were bred in aviaries.

In 1896, Mr. R. Phillips recorded that the female of a pair in his possession bit off pieces of bark approximately 4 inches (10 cm) in length, which were then folded in half and tucked in amongst her feathers with both ends sticking out. Six strips were often carried at a time, but the number varied. Any pieces which were dropped as the female entered the nest were ignored, and once inside she proceeded to chew and soften the bark. The sides of the box provided a support for the nest which was not interwoven, nor domed like the nests of White Eye-ringed Lovebirds. He found that additional pieces of bark were added after the eggs had been laid. If the twigs are provided fresh, the increased moisture should help to prevent unnecessary deaths in the shell caused by low humidity.

Peach-faced Lovebirds are today one of the most widely kept members of the genus. They have proved to be free breeders, but are very aggressive and pairs must be housed separately in aviaries. Even some true pairs do not agree outside of the breeding season, and a careful watch should be kept to ensure that no toes are mutilated following squabbles. When breeding, these lovebirds are far more amenable to each other, but the cock in particular may resent the chicks after they have left the nestbox. The youngsters should be separated as a precautionary measure from the adults as soon as they are eating independently, allowing the parents to go to nest again. However hens are quite likely to exhaust themselves if they are allowed to continue laying, and so no pair should be allowed to breed more than twice, or perhaps three times during a season, particularly when three or four chicks are reared in each round. Overbreeding of a reliable pair of lovebirds will lead subsequently to disappointing results. Peach-faced Lovebirds are regarded as the noisiest of the group, but in an outside aviary, their call should not cause great offence.

There are reports of budgerigars hatching and rearing Peach-faced Lovebirds successfully but such cases must be treated as exceptional. Reports of supposed cross-breeding with budgerigars are unlikely to be accurate, but Peach-faced Lovebirds have been hybridised with most of the more commonly available species of lovebird. Colour mutations have also been developed, and are now well established. The Pastel Blue form retains the pink face of the normal, but the colour is somewhat paler. The blue coloration is invariably deeper on the wings than the rest of the body. This mutation first appeared in Holland when a pair of normal Peach-faced owned by P. Habats produced two blue chicks, and a further one in the next round. The Yellow or Golden Cherry Lovebird is perhaps the most attractive Peach-faced mutation bred to date, with its vivid red head and throat and pale blue rump set against its golden yellow body colour. Masaru Iwata was the original breeder of the yellow mutation over twenty years ago.

A somewhat duller olive type has been bred in Australia, although it is still not common. As its name suggests, this mutation is darker than normal but the head remains red. The cobalt colouring of the rump region is darkened to slate. This mutation has proved useful in the development of other new colours. When paired with normals for example the Olives produce Jade Peach-faced Lovebirds. These are regarded as being more attractive than the olives. Their general body colour is jade green, the lower back is blue and the face is pinkish-red. The wings and back are of a sage green colour. One can but hope that these attractive mutations become more widely available over the next few years.

WHITE EYE-RINGED GROUP

This group is comprised of the remaining four members of the genus all of which will breed readily in captivity. It has in fact been suggested that the Fischer's, Masked, Nyasa and Black-cheeked Lovebirds are related subspecies, and this view is supported by the knowledge that crossings between these various types can yield fertile offspring. Imported stock is usually pure, because interbreeding between these forms is very rare in the wild. It is thought that these lovebirds evolved from a common ancestor and then became separated primarily as a result of volcanic and vegetational changes in their region.

NYASA LOVEBIRD – *Agapornis lilianae*. Shelley.
Reference: *Ibis*, page 466, plate 12. Date: 1894.
Source of original specimen: Liwondis, Upper Shiré,
    Malawi.
Alternative names: Lilian's lovebird; Nyasaland lovebird.

Distribution: Zambia, Malawi
and Rhodesia.

Length: 5 inches (13 cm).
Sexes: Similar in appearance. White ring around the eyes,
    characteristic of this group. Back and wings dark green,
    lighter and yellowish elsewhere apart from the head, neck
    and breast which are orange-red in colour. The red is
    more vivid on the head. Tail feathers are orange near the
    base with black barring. The beak is also red, the irides
    are brown while the feet and legs are greyish. Hens are
    supposed to be darker in colour, with more substantial
    beaks.
Young Birds: These are of a duller coloration than the adults.
Number of eggs and incubation period: Three to six eggs
    incubated for twenty-three days.

    The Nyasa Lovebird became known in 1864, but it was initially
identified as the Peach-faced Lovebird, although the latter does
not have the characteristic white eye ring. Shelley was to name
this new species after Miss Lilian Sclater thirty years after its
initial discovery. The confusion between the two varieties still
continued however, because when Nyasa Lovebirds were first
imported in 1926, they were despatched as a consignment of
Peach-faced. The difference was realised, and Mr. Seth-Smith

*Nyasa Lovebird (*Agapornis lilianae*).*

identified the species which had previously been unknown to aviculturists.

In the wild, these birds remain closer to water than other members of this group which are found in more arid regions. They range in small flocks of twenty or so birds at altitudes from 1,500–3,500 feet (450–1,050 metres), and although they occur as close as 50 miles (80 km) to the Black-cheeked Lovebird, the two forms do not actually overlap and there are no records of hybrids being seen in the wild. Fertile forms resulting from the crossing of these two species have however been bred in captivity.

Nyasa Lovebirds are not available very often these days which is unfortunate because they have much to recommend them as aviary birds. They have proved reliable breeders, although former attempts to establish them were handicapped by low fertility of the eggs. These birds can be kept on a colony system, which is unusual for lovebirds. There must be two nestboxes for each pair of birds, to reduce the risk of fighting in the colony. The boxes should all be positioned at the same height, and situated as far apart as possible.

All the white eye-ringed birds carry nesting material in their beaks, and Nyasa Lovebirds build the typical domed-shaped nest consisting of two chambers within their chosen box. They are often loathe to sample green food, but this should always be offered in the hope that it will be accepted. Additional supplements to the diet ought to be used if green food is ignored during the breeding season. The Nyasa Lovebird has gained a reputation for feather plucking. This behaviour could well be the result of a dietary imbalance which is more likely to appear when the birds are breeding. These lovebirds will readily accept sunflower seed, which is grown commercially, within their natural range but they should not be allowed to eat too much because their fitness will decline if they become overweight. An excess of sunflower seed to the exclusion of the other seeds in the mixture may underlie many cases of feather plucking.

Nyasa Lovebirds are said to make good foster parents for the offspring and eggs of other species of lovebird. An attractive lutino mutation was established but its numbers have fallen, following the general decline in the numbers of Nyasa Lovebirds kept in captivity. These birds can be safely wintered outside, once they are acclimatised.

BLACK-CHEEKED LOVEBIRD – *Agapornis nigrigenis*. W. L. Sclater.

Reference: *Bulletin of the British Ornithologists' Club*, page 61. Date: 1906.

Source of original specimen: Muguazi River, Zambia.

Distribution: Zambia.

Length: 5½ inches (14 cm).

Sexes: Similar in appearance. Darker green than Nyasa Lovebird, and in the Black-cheeked Lovebird, the red feathering of the head region is replaced by brown which merges into black on the cheeks. Orange-red feathering found at the nape of the neck and on the top of the breast. The beak is red, and white eye rings surround brown irides. The legs and feet are greyish.

Young Birds: Duller than the adults. Yellow irises.

Number of eggs and incubation period: Three to six eggs incubated for twenty-three days.

This lovebird was the last species to be discovered, as recently as 1904 by Dr. Kirkman. It has the most restricted range of any species, occupying a total of less than 5,000 square miles (12,800 sq. km.). The Black-cheeked Lovebird became a popular aviary inmate during the 1920's, and in 1929 alone, 16,000 of these lovebirds were caught in the space of only four weeks. This was achieved by scaring the birds from the sorghum crops so that they took to the trees which had been limed beforehand, and there was no escape for them.

Such irresponsible trapping led directly to a fall in their

127

*Black-cheeked Lovebird (*Agapornis nigrigenis*).*

numbers and with an export ban effective in Rhodesia these lovebirds are unlikely to become available again. Furthermore, repeated crossings of this species with the Nyasa Lovebird make it hard to obtain pure captive bred stock. Hybrid birds can be recognised by areas of plumage which have a reddish tint on the forehead, but even in a normal individual, there is a considerable variation in the depth of colour on the head.

The few pairs kept by breeders reproduce quite freely, and the Black-cheeked Lovebird is suitable for keeping in colonies providing the birds are housed in a large aviary. However although they are less aggressive than some other lovebirds, the Black-cheeked is unusual in that they are liable to attack their chicks before they are eating independently. When this happens it is likely that the adults want to breed again and resent the presence of the older chicks, which may need to be taken out of the nestbox or aviary somewhat prematurely. The decision can be very difficult to make, but if the parents have attacked their offspring previously, the safest policy is to remove the chicks when they are nearly fully feathered and hand feed them until they are accepting hard seed. It is not safe to return the chicks, or introduce new birds to a colony while the lovebirds are still breeding; the pecking order will be disturbed by the intrusion of the newcomers, and fights are inevitable. In addition, the remarks about nestboxes in communal aviaries outlined for the previous species are equally applicable to the Black-cheeked Lovebird.

The young lovebirds are not as colourful as the adults when they emerge from the nest. The variable amount of black coloration visible on the upper mandible of the beak disappears as the bird gets older. The irides also darken considerably, since they are yellow in a young Black-cheeked Lovebird and brown in a mature bird. It is now accepted that these lovebirds cannot be sexed by their eye colour which was previously thought to serve as a reliable guide. In an aviary, Black-cheeked Lovebirds are very active, and especially fond of bathing either in the rain or a shallow open water container. Failing this, they will be seen rolling around on wet green food, moistening their feathers.

FISCHER'S LOVEBIRD – *Agapornis fischeri*. Reichenow.
Reference: *Journal of Ornithology*, page 54. Date: 1887.
Source of original specimen: Ussure, Tanzania.

128

*Fischer's Lovebird (*Agapornis fische●

Distribution: North-western part of Tanzania, south of Lake Victoria.

Length: 5½ inches (14 cm).

Sexes: Similar in appearance. Basic colour green, yellower on the underparts, darker on the wings and back. Forehead is orange-red. Remainder of head olive, merging with orange on the cheeks and throat. Base of the neck also orange. Blue rump, tail green tipped with blue, mixed with orange and black. White eye ring, brown irides, the beak is red, the legs and feet grey.

Young Birds: Duller colouring than the adults, and have some black on their beaks.

Number of eggs and incubation period: Three to eight eggs which are incubated for twenty-three days.

The Fischer's Lovebird is found in a relatively arid area at a height of 3,500–5,500 feet (1050–1650 metres) above sea level. Grass seeds form the basis of their diet, and this species is often observed feeding on the ground. It has proved to be one of the most adaptable members of the whole genus and various colonies of these birds have sprung up following escapes from dealers. Fischer's Lovebirds were able to establish themselves for example at the port of Tanga on the coast of Tanzania. They also survived the rigours of wartime feeding better than any other species.

This and the following species are readily obtainable and true pairs should breed quite readily although there is the problem of sexing them correctly. The pelvic bone test mentioned earlier is useful for this group, since the bones become wider in the hen from January onwards. It is better to purchase a true pair which have bred together successfully in the previous year, even if it means paying a little more, rather than selecting odd birds. Fischer's Lovebirds can lay clutches of six or more eggs, and as domestication has proceeded, the number of eggs laid in each clutch has been increasing.

Almost any loose material such as old millet sprays and twigs in the aviary will be utilised for constructing the nest, since Fischer's Lovebirds are less fastidious about material than are members of the sexually dimorphic group. Some pairs may not appear to sit very tightly, but almost invariably the eggs hatch without problems. Most hen lovebirds probably do not begin serious incubation until at least two eggs have been laid and this means that the chicks are of a more even age when they hatch. The chicks open their eyes when they are about ten days old, and four days later the body feathers begin to emerge.

This species is very suitable as an introduction to the group, and is relatively inexpensive. These lovebirds are however spiteful birds, and must be kept apart in pairs. Adjoining aviaries should be double wired to prevent them attacking each other through the wire. They are robust birds and problems of acclimatisation are unlikely to arise because most Fischer's Lovebirds advertised for sale have been bred in this country. Fischer's are somewhat noisier however than most other species, with the exception of the Peach-faced and its call is often heard when the birds are on the wing.

Interbreeding has taken place with all other members of the white eye-ringed group and also the Peach-faced Lovebird, but every effort should be made to keep pure breeding stock free from hybrids. These birds are found in the wild only 40 miles (64 km.) from Black-masked Lovebirds but they remain separated because of the vegetation and terrain. The lack of overlap supports the theory that members of this group of lovebirds are closely related, but each developed in isolation because of geographical barriers. Mutations of Fischer's Lovebirds are now being bred, with the yellow form probably most widespread.

MASKED LOVEBIRD – *Agapornis personata*. Reichenow.
Reference: *Journal of Ornithology*, pages 40 and 55. Date:
    1887.
Source of original specimen: Serian, Tanzania.

*Yellow Masked Lovebird (*Agapornis personata*). Referred to as a Pied by some breeders, this has proved to be a recessive mutation.*

Alternative names: Black-masked Lovebird; Yellow-collared Lovebird.

Distribution: The Irangi district of North-east Tanzania. Range sometimes close to that of Fischer's Lovebird, but the two do not occur together.

Length: 5½ inches (14 cm).

Sexes: Similar in appearance. The head is dark brown, almost black but these lovebirds vary in their depth of colour. The wings are dark green, and the rest of the body is predominantly green, apart from the breast and the back of the neck which are yellowish, but may occasionally be more orange. The flight feathers are black, and the rump feathers are of a grey-blue coloration. White naked eye ring encircles brown irides, and the legs and feet are dark grey.

Young Birds: Are duller than their parents, and may have black visible on the upper mandible.

Number of eggs and incubation period: Three to six eggs incubated for about twenty-three days.

The Masked Lovebird is similar in habits to the preceding species, and has proved equally adaptable. The liberation of Masked Lovebirds at the coastal ports of Dar-es-Salaam and Tanga in 1928 has led to the development of flourishing colonies in these towns. Here they breed successfully under roofs of tile or corrugated iron, surviving the extreme heat of the midday sun.

In its natural environment, the Masked Lovebird, like Fischer's prefers to use tree holes as its nesting site, often adopting holes previously utilised by woodpeckers and barbets. They have been reported as breeding from January to August, but most

133

youngsters are hatched in May and June. This period coincides with the end of the rainy season when the grasses and other seeds on which the adults feed are swollen and ripening. Although Masked Lovebirds live in a somewhat arid region, the humidity is higher when the birds are breeding, and this point is vital for good breeding results with captive stock.

Black-masked Lovebirds have been bred many times in captivity, both in aviaries and cages, and colour mutations are now often kept. The Blue Masked form is the most widely known, but other colours including yellows (pieds), whites and more rarely cinnamons have also been recorded. In the Blue Masked Lovebird, the mask itself is not altered, but blue plumage occurs instead of the green seen in the Black-masked form, while the yellow feathering is replaced by white. The description of Blue Masked is perhaps rather confusing initially, until the birds have been seen or described.

Masked Lovebirds are quiet, but they cannot be trusted to breed regularly on a colony system, although this has sometimes been achieved without blood being shed, in a large aviary. It is safer therefore to house them in separate flights with access to suitable shelters. The young hatch with a covering of very thick red down, and birds of this species are usually reliable parents, but they must be left alone whenever possible. The risk of disturbance is invariably greater if the lovebirds are being bred in cages. Youngsters reared under these circumstances will benefit subsequently from access to a flight which enables them to develop their wing muscles fully.

Appendix 1

Bibliography

Arnall, L. & Keymer, I. F.
   1975 *Bird Diseases*, Baillière Tindall, London.
Bannerman, D. A.
   1951 *The Birds of Tropical West Africa* vol. 8. Oliver &
      Boyd, Edinburgh.
   1953 *The Birds of West and Equatorial Africa* vol. 1. Oliver
      & Boyd, Edinburgh.
Bates H. & Busenbark, R.
   Parrots & Related Birds, TFH. Pub. Inc., Neptune, NJ.
Forshaw, J. M.
   1973 *Parrots of the World*, Lansdowne Press, Melbourne.
Luke, L. P.
   1952 *Lovebirds and Parrotlets*, Cage Birds, London.
Roberts, A.
   1957 *The Birds of South Africa*, Capte Times Ltd.
Rogers, C. H.
   1975 *Encyclopaedia of Cage and Aviary Birds*, Pelham
      Books, London.
Rutgers, A.
   1972 *Encyclopaedia of Aviculture,* vol. 2, Blandford Press,
      Poole.
Soderberg, P. M.
   1977 *All About Lovebirds*, TFH Pub. Inc., Neptune, NJ.
Vane, E. N. T.
   1967 *Guide To Lovebirds & Parrotlets*, Iliffe Ltd, London.

Appendix 2

Useful Names and Addresses

Periodicals

American Cage-Bird Magazine, 3449 North Western Avenue, Chicago, Illinois, 60618, USA.

Cage and Aviary Birds, Surrey House, Throwley Way, Sutton, Surrey, SM1 4QQ.

Societies

USA. *The African Lovebird Society*, Box 142, San Marcos, California, 92069.

GB. *The Parrot Society*, Sec. N. D. Cooper, 17 De Parys Avenue, Bedford, Beds.

Appendix 3

Guide to Mutations and New Colours

Species	Mutation	Origin and Date
Red-faced	Lutino	Wild-caught
Madagascar	None	
Abyssinian	None	
Black-collared	None	
Peach-faced	Yellow (Golden Cherry)	Japan, 1954
	Yellow Pied	USA, 1960's
	Pastel Blue	Holland, 1963
	Olive	Australia, 1968
	Lutino	USA, 1970's
	Blue	Europe, 1977
Nyasa	Lutino	Australia, 1933
Black-cheeked	None	
Fischer's	Blue	South Africa, 1957
	Yellow	USA
Masked	Blue	Wild-caught
	Yellow/Pied	USA, 1935

The following colours have also been bred.

Species	Colour	Original Derivation
Peach-faced	Jade (Greywing, Pastel Light Green)	Normal × Olive
	Pastel Blue Pied	Pastel Blue × Pied
	Pastel Cobalt	Pastel Blue × Jade
	Pastel Mauve	Pastel Blue × Olive
	Cream-albino	Pastel Blue × Lutino
	White (Silver Cherry, Buttermilk)	Pastel Blue × Yellow
	Double Yellow	Yellow Pied × Yellow
Masked	White (Silver)	Blue × Yellow

Index

139

*Silver Cherry Peach-faced Lovebirds (*Agapornis roseicollis*).*